BROKEN DREAMS

A Survivor's Story

Ellen Benton Feinstein

To my daughters, Lisa and Ami,
so that they may finally know who their mother really is

In dreams, fears are never overcome;
the tormented are always stuck in slow motion.
Thane Rosenbaum, *Second Hand Smoke*

TIMELINE

Throughout this book, I have recounted an event that happened to me when I was very young -- generally during wartime and immediately after the war -- and then I have tried to relate it to the aftermath -- how the experience affected my thinking/feeling/acting many years later. Therefore, the narrative alternates back and forth between different time periods. The reader may find this confusing, so I have included this timeline as a reference to when the various events in my life took place as well as what was happening in the world around me.

1939
May 13: *The SS St. Louis sets sail from Hamburg, Germany, to Cuba with 937 refugees (mostly Jews) seeking asylum from Nazi persecution. They were denied entry to Cuba, the United States and Canada, and the ship had to turn back. They were finally accepted by various countries of Europe. After their return to Europe, more than a quarter of the ship's passengers died in concentration camps, in internment camps, in hiding or trying to evade the Nazis.*
September 1: *The German army invades Poland and World War II begins.*
September 4: *Warsaw is cut off by the German army.*
September 27: *Warsaw surrenders.*
September 29: *Nazis and Soviets divide up Poland.*
October : *The Warsaw ghetto is established.*
November (?): Ellen (Olga, Ola) is born in Drohobycz, Poland.
November 15: *The Warsaw Ghetto, containing over 400,000 Jews, is sealed off.*

1940
Month and date unknown: Ellen is given to a Polish family for safekeeping.

May 20: *A concentration camp is established at Auschwitz, Poland.*

1941
Summer: *Nazis break the Molotov-Ribbentrop Pact and invade eastern Poland.*
September 23: *Soviet prisoners of war and Polish prisoners are killed in Nazi test of gas chambers at Auschwitz in occupied Poland.*
December 7: *Japan attacks Pearl Harbor.*
December 11: *Germany declares war on the United States. The U.S. enters war in Europe.*

1942
Summer: *Swiss representatives of the World Jewish Congress receive information from a German industrialist regarding the Nazi plan to exterminate the Jews. They then pass the information on to London and Washington.*
Nazi extermination camps located in occupied Poland at Auschwitz, Birkenau, Treblinka, Sobibor, Belzec, and Majdanek-Lublin begin mass murder of Jews in gas chambers.
July 23: *Treblinka extermination camp opened in occupied Poland, east of Warsaw. The camp is fitted with two buildings containing 10 gas chambers, each holding 200 persons. Carbon monoxide gas is piped in from engines placed outside the chamber, but Zyklon-B will later be substituted. Bodies are burned in open pits.*
July 28: *Jewish fighting organizations established in the Warsaw ghetto.*

1943
April-May: *16 Jews in the Warsaw ghetto initiate resistance to deportation by the Germans to the death camps.*
April 19: *Waffen-SS attacks Jewish Resistance in Warsaw Ghetto*

April 19-30: *The Bermuda Conference takes place as representatives from the United States and Britain discuss the problem of refugees from Nazi-occupied countries. No action is taken with regard to the plight of the Jews.*
Spring: Bombing of house where Ellen is hidden.
November: *The U.S. Congress holds hearings regarding the U.S. State Department's inaction regarding European Jews, despite mounting reports of mass extermination.*

1944
January 24: The *War Refugee Board is established by President Franklin Roosevelt.*
March 24: *President Roosevelt issues a statement condemning German and Japanese ongoing "crimes against humanity."*
June 6: *The Allied Powers invade Normandy.*
August 4: *Anne Frank and family are arrested by the Gestapo in Amsterdam, then sent to Auschwitz. Later she is sent to Bergen-Belsen where she dies of typhus on March 15, 1945.*
German officers fail in an attempt to assassinate Hitler.
August 7: *The prisoners at Auschwitz-Birkenau rebel and blow up one crematorium.*
Okar Schindler saves 1200 Jews by moving them out of Plaszow labor camp.

1945
Nazis conduct death marches of concentration camp inmates ahead of the advance of Allied troops.
January 17: *Liberation of Warsaw by the Russians.*
January 27: *The Soviet army liberates Auschwitz.*
April 15: *The British liberate prisoners at Bergen-Belsen.*
April 29: *Troops from the United States liberate survivors from the Buchenwald and Dachau concentration camps.*
April 30: *Adolph Hitler commits suicide in his bunker in Berlin.*
May 7: *Germany surrenders and war in Europe is ended.*

Spring: Eda finds Ellen in home of Polish family.
Eda and Leon take Ellen to their home and begin adoption proceedings.
Summer: Eda takes Ellen to hospital for removal of adenoids.
Autumn: Eda and Leon decide to leave Poland; they hide in the home of a cousin in Krakow.
The family arrives in DP camp in Austria.
November 20*: The war crimes tribunal, composed of the U.S., Great Britain, France, and the U.S.S.R., is convened at Nuremberg, Germany.*

1946
Late spring: The family arrives in Gauting-bei-München, Germany, and moves into an apartment in theT.B. sanatorium where Leon works as a doctor.
Eda's brother Milek comes to live with us for a few weeks before emigrating to Australia.
Summer: The family rents a room in the home of the Heys.
Early autumn: Ellen starts first grade.

1949
September: Eda, Leon, and Ellen board the *General C. C. Ballou* and embark on their voyage to America.
The family moves into hotel(s) in uptown Manhattan.

1950
Spring: Ellen's first visit to a dentist.
Summer: Ellen goes to the Catskills with Uncle David and Aunt Genia
The family moves into a rent-controlled apartment.
December : Ellen stays with the Meyersons while Eda undergoes a mastectomy.

1951
Summer: Ellen goes to Camp Ranger.
The family moves to Clinton, NY, where Leon sets up a private practice.
Ellen starts seventh grade at Clinton Central School.

1957
June: Ellen graduates from Clinton Central School.
September: Ellen becomes a freshman at The University of Michigan.

1986
July: Eda and Leon arrive in St. Louis and move into Chesterfield Garden Villas.

1987
April 17: Leon dies.

2001
July 19: Eda suffers massive stroke.

2009
November 10: Eda dies.

Table of Contents

PREFACE

When the idea to write this book germinated in my mind, I intended to do extensive research so that I could be certain that all the facts were correct. However, the more I read and heard, the more confused I became about whether my reflections were my own memories or concepts I had acquired through my reading. Memories, especially the tenuous memories from childhood and the unpleasant ones we want to repress, are extremely fragile. As Marianne Fredriksson said in *Hannah's Daughters*, "She had realized there are only fragments, that 'memories' always consist of fragments the mind puts together into a pattern, adapts to a picture staked out early without the need for a connection with anything that really happened. A great deal is misunderstood by small children." That is why I have divided this memoir into those things that (I think) I remember and those that have been told to me by others.

A number of well-meaning people have urged me to read books and/or take classes on how to write, how to write a memoir in particular. The more I read, the more confused I became. Should I change the format or the sequencing? Should I cut some of the material or add more? I became so entangled in stylistic technicalities that I was no longer able to put any thoughts on paper. Reason prevailed when I asked myself what my objective was in writing this book. I came to the realization that my purpose is simply to tell my story as it flowed from my mind and my heart, without the imposition of formal regulations. I like to think of this as a literary counterpart of primitive art; it may ignore the rules of line, shading, and perspective, but it still manages to convey a world of feeling.

I make no claim to the irrefutable accuracy of the places, dates, and events presented here. I am simply trying to share with the reader my childhood memories and the bits and pieces of family history that I was able to glean, as perceived from the vantage point of this septuagenarian. I have also included quotes from a number of references I came across in the course of my reading because I find it reassuring that others share my thoughts and feelings and experiences -- that I am not alone.

PART I - I REMEMBER

The Earliest Years

My life is a lie. My mother and father are not the people who were present at my conception. My name is something I picked out of a Manhattan phone book. My birthday is not the real anniversary of the day I made my entry into this world. Even my status as an only child is not entirely accurate. No, I'm not in the witness protection program, nor am I an undercover agent or a spy. Nothing mysterious or glamorous. I am the product of consummate evil, a survivor of such monstrous cruelties that their devastation, more than sixty years later, still scars the lives of millions.

You may ask yourself, "Why would anyone want to write -- let alone read! -- another book about the Holocaust when so many have been written already?" I think it's for the same reason that we keep reading romance novels and war stories. Even if we know the outcome (Romeo and Juliet, Camelot), we never tire of telling and retelling these tales. The basic theme may be the same, but each person sees the events from a different perspective. It's like a group of people standing in a circle around a sculpture and trying to describe it to a blind man. Everyone is looking at the same statue, yet every person sees a slightly different part of it. The more descriptions he receives, the better will be the blind man's "vision" of the sculpture. Besides, people love stories. Long before we had written history, the continuity of civilizations was preserved through the stories that were passed down from generation to generation.

I was reluctant to write my history because everyone else's story seemed so much more interesting than mine.

Then I read this thought in Joan Anderson's *A Walk on the Beach*: "Everyone wants to hear the voice of someone who has gone through something real." Each of us, from the mightiest emperor to the poorest inhabitant of the tiniest village, embodies a fragment of history in his DNA and thus has a story that needs to be heard. So I will add my story to the mix in the hope that it will help future generations gain a better understanding of life during the Holocaust and its aftermath.

Why have I waited so long to write about all this? That is an integral part of the story. I could not make my memories public while my mother was still aware of the world around her because living under the Nazis made her so paranoid that she firmly believed that if the secrets she harbored were revealed, the authorities would come pounding on her door, drag her out of bed in the middle of the night, and deport her -- as well as me and my family -- to Siberia, or they would send us to prison, where we would be forced to do hard labor for the rest of our lives. No amount of reasoning could convince her that we were safe here in America. But we are dying out, we survivors, and lately I have realized that I, too, am getting somewhat long in the tooth. With increasing frequency, the words that are right on the tip of my tongue evaporate before I can get them out, and they don't come back to me for hours or days. So it seems the time has come to put these memories on paper.

My first real memory (at least it seems like a real memory to me rather than a figment of my imagination) is of lying in a baby carriage. In the background I see a deep blue-black, velvety sky studded with bright pinpoints of starlight. Over the handlebar of the carriage I see a face leaning toward me, smiling with her full mouth and her dark eyes. The face is round, framed by dark hair combed back on top and wavy at the sides, curling under just below the ears. How was I to

2

know that this would be the image of my mother I would carry around with me for the rest of my life?

This image is also the last memory I have of my life with my birth parents, except for one encounter with my biological father, which took place in a courtroom many years later when I was in college.

I was born one day (I don't know exactly which day) in November 1939, in Drohobycz, Poland. It was not an auspicious time for a Jewish baby to make her debut in that particular part of the world. Drohobycz is one of those towns that belonged to Poland one day, to Ukraine the next, then to Russia, then to Poland again. Mendelsohn gives an amusing illustration of this phenomenon in *The Found*: "There is a joke that people from this part of Eastern Europe like to tell, which suggests why the pronunciation and the spelling [of the name of the town] keep shifting: it's about a man who's born in Austria, goes to school in Poland, gets married in Germany, has children in the Soviet Union, and dies in Ukraine. *Through all that,* the joke goes, *he never left his village!*" Without being aware of it, when I started talking, I learned to speak in all three languages (Polish, Ukrainian, and Russian), and I suppose that's the reason I've always had a proficiency with languages. A few years ago Eda, my adoptive mother, said something that made me burst out laughing. When she asked me what was so funny, I told her that she had just uttered a sentence with five words, and each word was in a different language! Polish, Ukrainian, Russian, German, Yiddish, English, with a little French or Spanish thrown in for good measure -- all were fair game in our home. But regardless of which country claimed sovereignty over my birthplace, there was a marked lack of affection for Jews there. When World War II broke out, realizing that our chances for survival as a family were slim to none, my parents found a Polish Catholic family who -- for a substantial sum of money -- would take me in and hide and protect me, in the hope that at least I, the youngest member of our family, would somehow survive the war.

Except for the one dim memory of my birth mother pushing me in a baby carriage, I remember nothing about the time between my birth and the time I found myself with this Polish family. I don't even know the names of the Polish husband and wife who gave me shelter, so I will call them Stan (Stanislaw) and Anna. Probably I called them by the Polish equivalent of "mom" and "dad", although I have no idea how they managed the logistics of having a child suddenly appear in their home. I am certain that they went to great lengths to give the appearance of normalcy, since the slightest suspicion that they were harboring a Jewish (or gypsy or any other "undesirable") child would have put their lives in grave danger.

I knew they were not my real parents because I had a wallet-sized picture of my mother that I carried around with me for a long time. I don't know where I got that photo; perhaps my birth mother gave it to Anna to give to me when I was old enough to hold on to it. I also don't know what happened to that picture, but I wish with all my heart that I still had it today. However, I have always kept the image of that face in my mind, though over the years it has faded. Strangely, since I have been working on this book and have stirred up some long-buried contents of my subconscious, I had a dream last week. My mother and I were in a beautiful field of wildflowers. She was laughing joyfully as she chased a yellow butterfly, her long hair, becomingly dyed blond, flowing out behind her. And I said, "Now I know where I get my silliness!" Some little boys in the adjacent park threw a ball, which flew over the fence and landed close to my mother. She picked it up and threw it back with amazing force for such a small person. And I said, "Now I know where I get my strength." In my dream, the next morning at breakfast, my mother looked rather frumpy, with floppy slippers, a frayed bathrobe, frizzy brown hair, and no makeup. And I said, "I wish I had taken your picture yesterday when you were all dressed up. You looked soooooo lovely!" Apparently my psyche needs to be reassured that the genes my biological mother passed on to me endowed me with some good qualities.

Stan, my Polish Catholic "father," was a cobbler. When he was not drunk, he made and repaired shoes. I assume he had a shop somewhere, since he did not work at home. All I remember about this home is a front room with a cot in the front left corner where I slept, Stan and Anna's bedroom (all tiny and very sparsely furnished), and the basement. I'm sure there must have been a kitchen and a bathroom, but I can't picture these. The basement stands out in my mind -- a huge area with a gray concrete floor and a big ping-pong table in the middle and bars on the windows -- because that is where I spent so much of my time. There was also a small tool shed, which was always crammed with junk of all sorts. This shed played an important role during one of the bombings. But I'm getting ahead of myself, as frequently happens when you try to recapture memories that are not stored neatly in chronological order but that come tumbling out, all on top of each other.

I know that I must have played and interacted with other children, but I have no recollection of doing so. I have a vague memory of the anguish I felt when other children made fun of me because my head was shaved to get rid of lice. Apparently there was an outbreak of head lice and, while other children's mothers washed their hair in special solutions and picked through their hair to kill the nits, Anna chose the easy way out and shaved my head. It was not until I acquired my third mother (Eda) that someone took the trouble to kill the lice and save my hair. I remember answering the door in my nightgown, with my head shaved, barefoot in the dead of winter. The reason I was wearing a nightgown and walking barefoot in the dead of winter was that there was not enough money to buy me clothes and shoes. I was answering the door because angry customers, tired of waiting for their shoes to be repaired, were pounding on the door. Afraid to face these angry people, Stan and Anna made me open the door in the hope that this mob would not attack a little girl. The reason the shoes were not fixed was that whenever Stan got a few zlotys (Polish currency) in his pocket, he spent them on liquor.

I remember one evening when he came in, fell across the bed (I have no idea why the bed, stripped of sheets, was in front of the door. Maybe it had been moved there during one of the bombing raids), and vomited. This was not unusual, but what really upset me was that his false teeth fell out. Of course, I didn't realize they were false and I remember asking Anna over and over again, "But how will he chew? Will we have to mash up all his food from now on?" I was terribly concerned for Stan, and at the same time, I was fascinated by the way all his teeth fell out together. I knew that children lost their baby teeth, and I wondered whether all of mine would fall out at the same time the way his did. The next day I was relieved that his teeth had somehow grown back in his mouth and he was able to eat solid food again. Since Stan bought alcohol with whatever money he managed to collect during his sober working moments, there was not enough money for clothes and shoes. So instead of dressing me and feeding me, he and Anna kept me locked in the basement all day, naked, with a bowl of cottage cheese for nourishment. That's how I was when Eda found me at the end of the war in 1945.

I think it is important to explain that Stan and Anna were not cruel people, though when Stan was drunk, he was mean, and he and Anna fought bitterly. As a rule, they confined themselves to their bedroom during these fights, but sometimes they exploded into the "living room." One night Stan, shouting obscenities, chased Anna into the front room and urinated all over her nightgown while I watched in horror. I learned quickly to keep very still at those times and to make myself invisible in my little corner. Stan never touched me, but I am quite sure that if I had not been rescued until I was older, I would have been abused sexually, like those sad little girls who tell their stories in the stirring documentary *Diamonds in the Snow.* Stan and Anna had to leave me alone because there was no such thing as nursery school or baby sitters, and even if these had been available, there was no money for them. Mine was not a unique case. According to several accounts, families that took in Jewish children often kept them hidden in cellars or attics because if anyone became suspicious that a Jewish child was being sheltered, the entire family -- as well as the child -- would have been killed. Even though people must have been aware of my existence (the customers who came to the door when I answered it, the neighbors who shared our bomb shelter, other people who came to the house), I could not be left to wander around at will because I could not be trusted to stick to whatever story Stan and Anna used to explain my presence. I was not an obedient little girl, and I would not have stayed in the house. I had a mischievous streak, and I was not good at doing what I was told. So I'm sure they locked me up for my own protection. I am equally sure that this is a psychologically damaging way for a young child to spend her formative years.

But I know they were good to me because I have vague memories of Anna trying to comfort me during the bombings that occurred periodically from the time I was about three years old. The bombings -- how can I tell you what a ghastly ordeal they were for me? I would wake up in my little corner bed to the sound of the air raid siren, followed soon by the sound of hammering as Stan boarded up the windows with plywood in an effort to keep the glass from being shattered by the concussion from the exploding bombs. I would then have to get out of bed, use the bathroom, and hurry with Stan and Anna across the dark back yard, through an opening in the back fence and, after Stan lifted the cover, we would descend into a narrow tunnel in the ground until we reached a sort of man-made cave. Usually other neighbors would already be there. Try to envision a group of frightened people in the middle of the night, crowded into a cold, dark, fetid hole underground. I suspect that's how it would feel to be buried alive. I was not allowed to cry or make any noise. Only the adults sometimes talked in hushed whispers about what might be happening above ground. Their fear was evident in their voices, in their body language, in the smell of their cold sweat, in everything about them. Terror does not begin to describe my feelings at those times. We would stay in this shelter -- sometimes only minutes, sometimes for hours -- until the all clear sounded, then file back into our homes -- if we were lucky enough to still have a home to go to.

One episode does stand out in my mind with special clarity, for this time the drill occurred during daylight rather than the usual nighttime hours. We had been in the underground shelter for several hours when I just *had* to go to the bathroom. Stan and Anna pleaded with me to wait just a little longer, but I simply *had* to use the bathroom. Finally, Stan agreed to take me out of the shelter and into the house. As we started to head back, we suddenly heard the scream of warplanes approaching. We had gone too far to make it back to the shelter and we were still too far away from the house, so Stan pulled me into the tool shed, grabbed a steel bucket and a metal wash basin, put them over our heads, and pulled me down with him on the floor of the shed. There we were, the two of us, huddled face down amidst the rubble in the shed, with Stan's arm thrown protectively across my shoulders, when suddenly there was a series of tremendous explosions. The concussion shattered the panes in the small window, sending glass shards flying. Debris pelted our bodies and bounced against our improvised metal head coverings, causing them to resound deafeningly in our ears. Surely, between the urgency of my need and the terrible fear, I must have wet myself. It was all over in just moments, and then there was a strange silence.

We got up shakily, brushed ourselves off, walked out of the shed, and surveyed the landscape. There was rubble everywhere. The back of the house had been heavily damaged, and the back porch was reduced to splintered wood and broken glass. In dismay, Stan and I stood there looking, turned to each other -- and burst out laughing! Both of us must have felt an overwhelming relief at having survived such a close brush with death. Although it was a nightmarish experience, the memory of this episode always makes me feel contented and comforted. It's strange how the feelings associated with an event are sometimes completely at odds with the nature of the event itself. I think the reason I have such warm feelings when I recollect that frightening event is because of the close, almost loving human contact with Stan at that moment. Fear and shared relief wove us together with a common thread, and for the first time in my young life, I bonded with another human being. At age three, I was hungry for any scrap of caring, kind physical contact.

I would like to cite another example of this phenomenon. This event took place many years later, after we had arrived in New York in 1949. I must have been about ten years old when Eda went into the hospital for a few days to have a mastectomy. According to what she tells me, she did not have a malignancy, only a large fluid-filled cyst in her breast. In those days (1950), treatment was much more aggressive and radical; when she had the same condition in the remaining breast several years later, they simply aspirated the fluid. At any rate, Leon, her husband, had to spend time with her in the hospital (in those pre-HMO days they kept you in the hospital for several days after surgery) and I was too young to be left home alone, so they farmed me out to some distant cousins, the Meyersons, who lived in the Bronx.

I don't remember much about the rest of the family, but I do remember the daughter named Rita. She must have been a junior or senior in high school at the time, and I thought she was the most beautiful person I had ever seen, with her

9

sparkling dark eyes and her tall, slim figure. Rita had endless patience with me, and she used her artistic talents to make costumes for paper dolls for me; these are dolls drawn on the soft cardboard covers of books, which you can cut out with scissors. Inside the books are paper pages with costumes that can also be cut out. Each of the costumes and accessories has tabs sticking out, which you bend over behind the doll to hold the garment in place (it took me a few mistakes to learn not to cut off the tabs or the clothes would be useless). Nothing in my life has ever fascinated me more and has held my attention for more hours than these dolls with their variety of costumes, both the ones in the books (Rita bought me a couple of these) and the ones she made for me. We spent countless hours dressing and undressing these dolls, accessorizing their outfits with miniature gloves and tiny hats and shoes, tabbing jackets and sweaters and coats over their dresses until the dolls grew so bulky that the clothes would no longer stay on.

Rita made me feel that she enjoyed spending time with me. She talked to me about school and boys, she fixed my hair, she taught me how to play checkers and Chinese checkers. She was the first person who ever read me a story at bedtime. It was Christmas week and for once, there was clean white snow on the city streets. Rita went for walks with me to show me the lovely decorations, and we threw snowballs at each other and shrieked with laughter. I worshiped Rita. For the first time in my life, I was having a good time with someone who was close to my age, and a very guilty part of me hoped that Eda would leave me there forever.

And then came Saturday night, December 23, the day before Christmas Eve, and Rita had a date. While the whole world was celebrating the holidays, I was left alone (Rita's parents stayed in the apartment, but they paid no attention to me), abandoned by the only person who had ever made me feel that she actually liked being with me. From the moment

Rita walked out the door with her date, looking more gorgeous than ever, I got that empty, blue, hollow-chested, lump-in-my-throat, weepy feeling -- the same feeling I now get when my daughters leave after a visit and I walk into their empty rooms. All evening long the radio played *Have Yourself a Merry Little Christmas*, over and over and over again. Even today I can't listen to that song without getting that same blue, weepy feeling, and I can't sing along to it without choking up. So although the week I spent at the Meyersons' was one of the happiest times in my life up to that point, incongruously the feeling evoked by the memory is that of a bittersweet sadness.

In a similar way, whenever I recollect the terror of the day when the bombs came so close to killing Stan and me, I feel an incongruous sensation of warmth and comfort because of the common bond between Stan and myself at that moment.

Did these experiences scar me for life? Who can say? I am not claustrophobic, nor am I afraid of the dark, as one would expect. On the other hand, the sound of a civil defense siren can produce a visceral response in me, sending goose-bumpy shivers all through me. I am not afraid of lightning, even though I know that is the dangerous component of a thunderstorm, but I have an irrational fear of the sound of thunder. And decades later, when I was an adult living in Galveston, I insisted that we have a carpenter make up a set of plywood shutters that fit on the outside of our large windows with a cumbersome set of hooks and eyes, instead of boarding up the windows with plywood the way our neighbors did every time there was a hurricane threat. Even the sound of the hammering from neighborhood houses made me cover my ears with a pillow, uneasy about more than the imminent storm.

One day in 1945, when I was about five years old, as I was playing my lonely games in the basement, a face appeared at the window above me. It was a rather pretty, dark-haired lady, and she started speaking to me. I wasn't particularly interested until she held a Hershey bar through the bars on the window. Hurriedly I pulled a chair over to the window, climbed on the chair, and snatched the candy out of the lady's hand. Although a small warning voice at the back of my head told me that I shouldn't be taking it, there was no way I was going to pass up that heavenly treat! (I don't know how I knew what it was or how it would taste, since I don't recall ever having had a chocolate bar before; maybe the love of chocolate is an inborn trait?) It seems to me that she said something about being my mother, which confused me somewhat, but how can a question of mere motherhood compete for attention with a Hershey bar with almonds?! I have a mental picture of myself: a skinny naked little kid with a round face and a shaved head, tearing into that candy bar like a starving wild animal. It's a wonder Eda didn't turn on her heels and leave me there. But she had promised her dying sister that she would take care of her little girl if both of us should survive the war and miraculously find each other again.

Life With Eda and Leon in Poland

I have no recollection of the transition from Stan and Anna's house to Eda and Leon's apartment. I don't even know in what city it was located. I picture a room with two windows, draped in rich burgundy velvet curtains; the fancy gold tiebacks were never used because the drapes were always pulled tightly together, shielding the view from inside and from outside. My overall impression is of a dark room filled with dark wood furniture and beautiful trinkets, but to a five-year old who was raised in bare subsistence, the look was one of wealth and good taste. Eda told me that on one occasion, she saw two soldiers knocking on doors and entering the apartments. She knew that if they got into our apartment, they would take away all the valuables. So she told me to stay quiet, and when the soldiers knocked on our door, she went out into the hallway, shutting the door behind her, and convinced them that there was a child inside who was very sick with a communicable disease; thus she was able to save our belongings by using her wits.

At first Eda and Leon told me that they were my real mother (*matka*) and father (*ojciec*). After some time, they told me to call them Aunt (*Ciocia*) Eda and Uncle (*Wujek*) Lonek. I learned much later that when Eda found me, she and her husband Leon (Lonek, as Eda called him) already had their precious visas to come to America. Because they didn't have any papers to show that I was their legal ward, they had to go through the adoption procedure and then try to get new visas, an extremely difficult process because the U.S. was not exactly greeting Jewish refugees with open arms. Contrary to the general impression that America welcomed the "huddled masses," the National Origins Quota of 1924 -- which limited the number of immigrants allowed into America to no more

13

than 2% of the number of each nationality residing in the U.S. in 1890 -- was still in effect, severely restricting the number of Jews allowed into this country. To receive a visa, you needed to have a sponsor who would guarantee your financial solvency and you had to be in a profession that was considered essential. Entry visas were almost impossible to obtain, and it was unthinkable that someone would give up a visa and remain in a country where Jews were despised and were frequently taunted and sometimes even shot simply out of hatred. For this unfathomable sacrifice, I will always owe Leon and Eda a debt greater than anything I could ever do to repay them. To a large extent, being aware of this debt has helped me deal with many of the conflicts I've had with Eda. I bit my tongue and kept my angry thoughts to myself because I always told myself that I could do at least this much for her. Of course, it was like an albatross around my neck, a constant source of guilt for me. Helen Fremont expressed my feelings perfectly in her book *After Long Silence*: "...I know what it is ... to receive the gift of sacrifice, to spend a life swimming in a fishbowl of guilt, looking frantically for a way to break through the glass."

During the period I lived with them in Poland, they always took me with them to adult functions, since babysitters were either unavailable or unaffordable. After the initial pleasantries, I was expected to sit quietly and entertain myself (the old "children should be seen and not heard" routine). Since I was accustomed to entertaining myself, this was not too hard for me. But I did devise one strategy that caused Eda no end of embarrassment. I would case the living room and zero in on one target, usually a piece of bric-a-brac in a display case. Then I would make such a show of admiring this object that the hostess felt compelled to insist that I take it. I acquired a number of treasures in this way. The prettiest was a little porcelain figurine of a blonde girl wearing a flowered hat, a blue bodice, and a full multi-flowered skirt swinging out over ruffled pantaloons trimmed with lace, all executed with

14

such delicacy that I am amazed that I didn't break it immediately, unaccustomed as I was to handling fine things. The first time I used this ploy, I was simply admiring something pretty in one of the homes, but I quickly realized that I had a winning gimmick. Whenever Eda berated me after we got home, with my ill-begotten prize of the evening clutched to my chest, I would reply with mock innocence, "But I didn't ask her to give it to me. I was just being polite and telling her how much I liked it."

Shortly before I turned six, a pivotal incident took place that had a profound impact on my life-long emotional development, my relationship with Eda, and my enduring code of ethics. Apparently I had been prone to frequent upper respiratory and inner ear infections. One day Eda dressed me in my only good dress -- which she had starched and pressed carefully -- and my stockings, tied a big bow in my hair with great care, and told me that we were going to a birthday party. I was giddy with anticipation. We climbed onto the back of an army jeep, the most common mode of transportation, and drove for a long distance over bumpy mud tracks. And then the jeep pulled up in front of a hospital. The next thing I remember is lying on an operating table and having an ether mask (sort of like a catcher's mask padded with pink cotton and soaked in ether) clamped over my face. I fought with all my might, but I was being restrained. The smell was making me nauseous and I couldn't breathe, I felt like I was suffocating, and I knew I was going to die.

When I woke up, my throat was terribly painful and I was vomiting blood; my adenoids had been removed. Eda was sitting by my bedside but I could barely stand to look at her. What an overwhelming sense of betrayal! The earth had opened up beneath me and swallowed my fledgling faith in the goodness and honesty of people. To look forward to the pleasure of the promised party and to wake up like this! Though I was not able to articulate what I felt, I sensed that I would never again have confidence in her word. This deception, this betrayal by the person I was just learning to trust and depend on, was more destructive to me than all the horrors of the war. Once more, the foundation beneath me had shifted, and I felt somehow that my feet would never again find solid ground. Eda could not understand this because she believed it was OK to tell little white lies to spare someone's feelings or to keep them from being scared or worried. I strongly disagree with her. I believe firmly that once you find out that someone has lied to you, your trust in that person is broken forever and you can never again take what she or he tells you at face value. This belief is something I have stressed to my daughters from the time they were very small: the worst thing you can ever do to someone you love is to be dishonest, no matter how small the fib or how noble your motives. My husband and I have had many contentious battles over this concept. Whenever he has forgotten or neglected to do something he promised to do, I tend to overreact. To his way of thinking, "What's the big deal? So I didn't mail the letter/get the car washed/pick up the papers. Nothing bad happened. Life goes on." In my eyes, it's "another broken promise. How can I ever trust him to keep his word in the future?" If I make a promise to you, you can be sure that I will not break that promise.

To be fair to Eda, I was not an easy child to deal with. I had grown up like a little animal, undisciplined, uneducated in the finer points of human interaction, uncared for, unloved. Eda did her best to tutor me in all these areas. She even taught me the rudiments of reading and writing. Teaching me to write the alphabet was quite a challenge. When we got to the letter "g," I dug in my heels and cried impatiently, "I'll never learn this! I'm not going to try anymore!" But Eda prevailed, and eventually I did manage to master the Polish alphabet.

You may have noticed that I have not mentioned Leon in any of these interactions. There is a good reason for that.

Leon was an extraordinary man who could win over even the meanest, grumpiest, least tolerant individuals. He was a gentleman in the truest sense of the word, but he was a quiet, soft-spoken man who was content to retreat into the background and let Eda do all the talking. My daughters and I still laugh about one particular incident. Eda and Leon used to call us every week when we lived in Galveston and they lived in upstate New York. We would each get on an extension and everyone would take turns talking and listening -- everyone, that is, except Eda, who always did the talking. One day she paused and offered uncharacteristically, "Lonek, why don't you say something?" There was a slight pause, and then Leon said sheepishly, "Now that I have the floor, I don't know what to say." But don't get the false impression that he was not smart and witty. Whenever Leon made a remark, it was always something that was appropriate to inject at that point in the conversation, never unkind, always clever. The girls used to fight for the privilege of sitting next to him at the dinner table so that they could hear his *sotto voce* commentary on the conversation.

Let me illustrate my relationship with him by telling you about another of my recollections. In the south of Poland, at the foot of the Tatra Mountains was a ski resort town called Zakopane. We went there once for a short vacation, and I remember hiking on one of the gorgeous snow-capped mountains. I have a vague sense that we were with other people -- friends of Eda and Leon's. What I remember clearly is my astonishment that even though we were walking in the snow, the sun was warm on our bodies and we didn't need our coats. Until then I had always associated snow with bitter cold. I may have been strong-willed, but I was not a strong child physically (small wonder, considering that I had spent my early years malnourished and without any physical exercise). It was not long before I tired and couldn't climb any farther. Leon picked me up and carried me on his shoulders. Eda trotted at his side, fussing and fretting that I was too

17

heavy and that he would get a hernia, but he ignored her and carried me the rest of the way, which could not have been easy for him. There have been numerous references in literature to the joyful, powerful feeling a child experiences riding on a father's shoulders. To me this meant much more: it was an affirmation that even though he customarily deferred to Eda, I could always count on Leon's quiet strength when I really needed it.

By this time I had started thinking of Eda and Leon as my parents (*rodzici*). I began calling them mama and daddy (*tatus*) when Eda told me that they truly were my real parents. Many years later, when I asked her why I was told to call them "aunt" and "uncle" at first, she said it was only because of the legal requirements for getting a visa to emigrate. She got one of those funny little smiles on her face that she always had whenever she was not being truthful, and she told me that someday I would understand. That was a ploy she used to the very end: any time she didn't want to explain something to me, she would say that someday I would understand. That "someday" has never arrived because there are still a great many things I don't understand. Although I had my doubts about what she told me (I still carried around the mental image of my biological mother), I wanted so badly to have parents, to belong to someone, that I didn't challenge her. She perpetuated this falsehood until the time I was in college, when my biological father resurfaced and she was forced to tell me the truth. Eda spent several sleepless nights trying to figure out how to break the news to me without shattering me emotionally. She was surprised that I was not surprised.

From the time I came to live with them in 1945, my parents had very different styles of disciplining me. Eda used lectures, oblique references, little morality stories, histrionics, guilt, nagging -- any tool at her disposal to manipulate me into doing what she wanted. Whenever I asked for something, Eda's immediate response would be "no." It didn't take me long to figure out that if I persisted long enough, she would eventually give in, but she would not do so graciously. On the other hand, Leon would ask a few pertinent questions and if my answers were satisfactory, he would usually grant me his permission. However -- and here's the big difference -- if in his judgment my request was inappropriate and he said "no," that was the end of the story. I knew that no amount of pleading, wheedling, or arguing would make him change his mind. I had great respect for his reasonable approach and his adherence to his principles. Eda could rant and call me names and tell me how foolish my opinions were, and my response would be, "You just don't understand!" Leon could bring me to my knees with just a gentle, "You're a silly billy."

There is another occasion that -- even though it occurred many years later -- demonstrates my father's direct way of dealing with me. When we came to America in 1949, I needed to have some dental work done. Not only had I never heard of fluoride during my formative early years, but my diet lacked the basic nutrients, and I don't remember ever having seen a toothbrush; we simply rinsed our mouths with water after eating. In New York, my father took me to an acquaintance from Europe who was a dentist. Seated in the big dentist chair, I suddenly became so scared that I clamped my jaws shut. No amount of coaxing could convince me to open my mouth. When the dentist tried to pry my jaws open, I bit his finger so hard that I drew blood. I didn't mean to be bad, I was just scared. After we left the dentist's office, while we were waiting for the bus to take us home, my father said grimly, "Boy, are you going get it when we get home!" And I thought to myself, "I'm going to have to go back and get this done at some point anyway. So why get a spanking and make daddy mad and make mother upset? I might as well go back right now and get it over with." I asked my father to take me back, and I faced the ordeal like a trooper. Even today, so many years later, whenever I'm confronted with a task that I really don't want to do, I think of this incident and I tell myself, "You might as well get it over with instead of procrastinating and having it hanging over your head and maybe even paying a penalty for not getting it done on time."

No, I was not an easy child to deal with. Meal times were a daily battleground for Eda and me. You would think that after so much deprivation, so much real hunger -- at times even bordering on starvation -- I would be ravenous for any food I could get my hands on. But that's not how it was. My taste buds had never developed an appreciation for fine flavors, and my system had never developed a tolerance for any sort of quantity or variety. Trying to build up my strength, Eda would go to a great deal of trouble to obtain and prepare dishes that she thought I would enjoy. She would coax me and feed me like a little child, one spoonful at a time. She would fall asleep at the table, wake up, reheat my food, and start again. More often than not, by the time I had finished eating what she had prepared, everything would come up again. Most discouraging! She tried to boost my immune system by making me swallow a tablespoon of cod liver oil every morning. What a horrible ordeal! I gagged and wretched violently, and the oily coating and fishy taste would stay in my mouth all day, even after I had brushed my teeth. For many years, I was unable to eat any fish without becoming intensely sick to my stomach, and I still can't stand any fish that's oily or has a strong flavor.

Food was an issue repeatedly during my childhood. The final episode with my picky eating happened after we had moved into our apartment in New York City. Eda served tomato soup with rice, and there was no way I was going to eat *that*! Leon had had enough of this nonsense and decided to end this manipulation on my part once and for all. The bowl of tomato soup sat on the counter and then in the refrigerator, and I was not allowed to touch anything else until I finished it. My hunger strike lasted for two and one-half days with nothing except water crossing my lips. Eda was hysterical. Dad insisted that "no child has ever starved to death willingly. When she gets hungry enough, she'll eat it." After almost three days, anything would have tasted good, and I finally broke down and devoured the tomato soup. From that moment on, I was no longer a picky eater. In fact, now I like all foods so much that I have to restrain myself from overeating and gaining weight.

Leon was a physician. He was what today would be the equivalent of a board certified radiologist. (In those days, he was known as a "roentgenologist," since "Roentgen" is the German word for "X-ray," named after its discoverer, Wilhelm Roentgen, a German physicist.) Since tuberculosis was quite prevalent at the time around World War II, his profession was held in high esteem and was in constant demand. He often traveled to Zakopane (a resort town at the foot of the Tatra Mountains, which was known for its antituberculitic sanatorium and its hydrotherapeutic institutions [spas], all of which were closed down after World War II) to serve as a consultant and a teacher.

Eda's job was to take care of the household and of me and to serve as a decorative element on Leon's arm. The former function she performed because it was expected of her; the latter she executed with relish. Petite, stylish, and charming, she basked in the status accorded to her as Mrs. Dr. Zwilling (later Benton). Her social gatherings, with the artistic flourishes she imparted to everything she served, were legendary. Throughout her life, elegance was her hallmark.

After I had lived with them for about six months, Eda and Leon, realizing that there was no chance that we would ever get to America from Poland because Polish émigrés were not being admitted, decided to leave Poland. Roosevelt had turned away a ship filled with Jews from Poland, who then had to go to Israel, because the quota was filled. My parents had heard that Jews could go to Germany and that it was easier to get into the U.S. from there. Eda has told me that when we were trying to flee Poland, a distant cousin hid us in his home in Krakow. While we were there, a neighboring woman, who didn't realize we were Jewish, remarked one day, "Jews are sprouting up everywhere like mushrooms." I know this woman's words made a lasting impression on Eda because she repeated them to me several times. Under the blanket of silence that followed the war, hatred for the Jews did not diminish, and many atrocities continued to take place.

Thus began our long journey in search of freedom and a better life, though we would have to suffer through much privation before we embarked on the home stretch.

Transition

And so we filled a couple of small suitcases with the essentials and, like the proverbial refugees with nothing but the clothes on their backs, we started our journey. It was dark when we arrived at the railroad station and boarded a train bound for Czechoslovakia. As you can imagine, we did not ride in first class! We were packed into a freight car with a mass of other people trying to escape. No seats, no sanitation facilities, no windows, no air. Just the dirty floor of the boxcar and the huddled, frightened people headed for an uncertain destination. I have only a dim memory of our travels, the first part of a harrowing ordeal. Only one episode stands out in my mind.

Refugees were not allowed to bring any valuables across the border, and if they tried to carry anything of value, it would most likely be stolen or confiscated. Afraid of being completely destitute, Eda sewed a few small gold nuggets into the lining of my coat. She told me it was for some dental work that she needed, but I suspect it was intended as a bargaining/bribery chip in case the need arose. We arrived at the Czech border in the middle of the night and were unloaded from the train. Each of us was then searched thoroughly by the border guards, who were very intimidating with their uniforms, their rifles, and their barked orders. They finished searching the three of us and waved us on. I turned to my mother and said in my loud, piping little voice, "See, I told you they wouldn't find anything on me." The guard turned back toward us, my mother turned white and gasped, my father's eyes opened wide in terror. At that instant I knew I had done something very bad. Instead of pointing his rifle to shoot us, as we fully expected at the time, the guard gave a small wink, turned back, and started walking away.

I was a child and didn't understand that my slip of the tongue could have had fatal consequences for all of us. But as Henry Roth quotes his mother saying: "A *mensch* is a *mensch*, *goy* or Jew." Every race, every nation, every group, almost every family consists of good people, not so good people, and downright evil people. That is why I have little empathy for those who lump together an entire race or nationality and assign stereotyped characteristics to them. I can't empathize with Jews who refuse to buy any German-made product or a Japanese car because of what the Germans and the Japanese did during the war. It's a natural tendency to lay blame at someone's doorstep; after all, that's how the Jews came to be persecuted in the first place. I know that there were kindhearted Germans and Poles who risked their lives to help victims and, sad to say, there were greedy Jews who informed on their *landsmen* for personal gain.

It's true that during the war a mass mentality prevailed that united the German people in a hatred of the Jews, and in this context I refer to "the Germans" or "the Poles" as a unified entity. This wartime phenomenon is common to all nations: a people united in hatred of the enemy, a hatred whipped up by propaganda and by the fact that "our boys over there" are being killed by the enemy, whoever the enemy may be at the time. Although America has not been subjected to international conflict on its shores (9/11 was not a prolonged conflict on American soil), one has only to witness the internment of the Japanese, many of whom were loyal American citizens, in prison camps (as described so poignantly by David Guterson in his novel *Snow Falling on Cedars*) to recognize how easily a nation can be goaded into a mentality of hatred. Or think about the Civil War: brother ready to kill brother, the North pitted against the South, one group of people ready to kill those whom they embraced just before the madness took hold. And each side believed that the cause for which it was fighting was just and righteous.

Someone once said that war does not determine who's right, the only thing war determines is who's left. How true! One of the most disturbing aspects of war and the one that is most difficult to comprehend during peacetime when life follows a pattern is the complete disorientation of time, place, and person that occurs. The film *Europa Europa* gives some excellent insights into the capricious, arbitrary, unpredictable way life changes from moment to moment. The protagonist puts up his hands to surrender, fully convinced that he is going to die, and instead, he is credited with winning an important battle and becomes a hero in the German military. He drifts from place to place, never knowing whether the kind lady in whom he confides, out of his need to talk to someone, will turn him in as soon as he walks away. That's the way it is during wartime. You are perpetually kept off balance, and logical thinking and planning are virtually impossible. There is no support system, no safe haven to which you can retreat for a time-out, it's not possible to distinguish -- other than the obvious uniforms and Hitler salutes (and some of those were faked as well for self-preservation) -- who is friend and who is foe. Time has no meaning, nothing makes any sense. You exist in a kind of limbo, wandering from place to place, trying to stay hidden, reacting only to danger from any source -- including starvation (I have heard of people fighting aggressively over little bits of plant roots dug up from the frozen ground). If there were a way to know when and how the war was going to end, it would be much easier to endure; it's the uncertainty that makes it so unbearable.

After passing through Czechoslovakia, we wound up in a camp for displaced persons (DPs) in Austria. These camps were set up by the United Nations Relief and Rehabilitation Administration (UNRRA) in several European countries for the 250,000 refugees fleeing persecution in their native land and hoping to find a better life elsewhere. Ravaged by the long war, these countries were able to provide only the barest necessities for these "huddled masses." "Displaced persons"-- what a genteel euphemism for souls in limbo, for emaciated bodies that nobody knows what to do with! A large number of people were packed dormitory-style into makeshift tent-like structures. The mattresses on the floor were only a few feet apart. The plumbing was woefully inadequate and there was no heat. In these appalling conditions, infectious diseases were frequently passed from person to person and back again. Medications were scarce. Rats and head lice were commonplace. Often Eda would run a fine-toothed comb through my hair and pick through my scalp for nits, which she would squash between the nails of her thumbs (she was always adept at nitpicking, both literally and figuratively!).

My parents tried to get to Ulm, where Eda's brother Milek (Samuel) was the director of a DP camp, but because of the harsh weather, they were forced to stay in the camp near Vienna. The most dreadful memory for me is standing in the food line. It was an especially severe winter, and we did not have sufficient warm clothing or footwear. We stood for hours (at least, it seemed like hours), single-file, in a queue that stretched on and on, each of us -- including the very young, the very old, and the infirm -- holding a wooden bowl and a spoon. When we finally reached the head of the line, a skimpy amount of soup -- a thin, watery liquid with some fat "eyes" and a few minuscule pieces of unidentifiable vegetables floating in it -- was ladled into our bowls from a huge kettle heating over an open fire. Not exactly gourmet cuisine, but at least it was warm, or sometimes only tepid. This and a piece of bread were our daily staples.

Henry Cohen, the Director of Camp Foehrenwald in Germany, describes the conditions in one DP camp and the attitude of the American soldiers as follows (even though this camp was in Germany, similar conditions existed in Austria): "Many of you are not aware of the moderate, but distinct, anti-Semitism that existed in the United States in the 1930s and

1940s when I was growing up. The anti-Semitism often manifested itself in our relations with the American occupying force. The United States Army, particularly at the local level, was responsible for maintaining order in Germany. Many officers were unsettled by the population flows. In a rather strange way many of the soldiers on the ground felt more comfortable with the defeated Germans than they did with the unkempt Jewish survivors. 'There have been numerous incidents involving Jewish DPs. ...This, in its turn, has a definitely bad effect on the German population, who, when conscious of such situations, rather incline toward their belief Hitler was not such a bad judge of the Jew, after all.' ...These were American officers writing these lines in 1946. ...[T]he lack of understanding and empathy on the part of these American officers is, to this day, beyond my comprehension. ...The anguish of survival was etched on everyone's face: the persisting painful memories of relatives and friends killed; the horrendous memories of one's own survival experience; the sight of children quiet and unsmiling. Managing the Camp was often impossibly difficult. In January, when the camp was most congested, a Bavarian frost froze the pipes and resulted in the complete or partial damage to 400 of the 600 toilets in the camp. The sanitary conditions in the toilets was appalling. A month or two later, explosives at the I.G. Farben plant cracked open the main pipe line bringing water to the Camp. For five days the camp was without water. No plumbing, no drinking water. No hot food could be cooked. The hospital was without water. The army provided merely token assistance. ...There was a black market in food. The army at the field level was obsessed with the black market and the number of Jews involved in it. Actually the numbers of Jews involved was small, and considering the quality of the food we were serving, it would have been surprising if there were no efforts to improve it."

From time to time, the Bakenroders, friends of my parents from Poland, sent powdered eggs and powdered milk to provide me with some nourishment. I couldn't stand the taste or the consistency of those powdered eggs -- they made me gag. On rare occasions a care package, sent by cousins in France who had heard of our situation, actually reached us. These packages contained fabrics and clothing and food, and one contained a sealskin coat for Eda to keep her from freezing during that cold winter. Sometimes these packages contained real eggs, sometimes cheese or other tidbits. The eggs and all the nourishing items were always given to me. Not once did my parents eat one of those precious eggs, though I'm sure they were very tempted. Although Eda was always hungry, from time to time she gave a little of the food we received to Leon so that he could keep on performing his duties as the camp doctor.

This unselfishness on their part has become symbolic for me of all the sacrifices they made on my behalf. It goes without saying that I am everlastingly grateful to them for having saved me and protected me to the best of their ability, but it also saddled me with an immense burden of guilt. How could I ever repay them? How could I be worthy of all their sacrifices by living up to their (especially Eda's) impossibly high expectations of me? How could I ever deny them anything or hurt them or make them angry? On the other hand, how could I be perfect? Whenever I let them down, the guilt I felt was overwhelming, and I spent most of my growing-up years berating myself for being such an ungrateful, heartless, inconsiderate, insensitive, lazy, obstinate, incorrigible daughter, a belief that was often reinforced by Eda's caustic comments and harsh judgments. In many subtle -- and often not so subtle -- ways, she never let me forget the sacrifices she had made for me.

During the six months we spent in this camp, there were a few bright moments. Once my parents took me to Vienna (I don't know the circumstances behind this ride in a military vehicle), where I saw Sonja Henie skating in an outdoor rink. It was my first encounter with something so beautiful in the midst of the squalor to which I was accustomed, and I was enthralled. The city, the buildings, the shops, the trees, the open spaces, the flawless grace of this gifted skater were almost more than I could take in, and I felt as if I would burst with emotions I couldn't express.

Since education is of vital importance in Jewish life, schools were set up and teachers came from other countries, including Israel and America. Along with a few other children in the camp, I attended a makeshift Hebrew school taught by one of these teachers. My native ability with languages stood me in good stead, and in no time at all I was prattling in Hebrew. I remember coming back to our barracks one day and announcing to my parents that since we were Jewish, we should be speaking Hebrew, not German. That didn't last long. At holiday time, the Hebrew school decided to put on a little skit for the parents. I was to sing a solo as part of the play. Everything went fine during rehearsals, and I warbled out my song in my little high-pitched child's voice like a pro. Then came the night of the play, and suddenly there was an audience out there. I walked onto the stage, took one look at the audience, and froze. I curled one leg behind the other, stuck my index finger in my nose, and just stood there until they had to carry me off bodily. So much for a career on the stage!

True, the living conditions in the displaced persons camp were harsh, but they were certainly better than in the concentration camps. We were being warehoused, but we were not being exterminated.

I don't remember making the trip, but I do know that after six months in the DP camp, we were able to leave Austria and continue on the next leg of our trek, once more traveling by train.

Germany

From the time in 1946 when we arrived in the small hospital/sanatorium for tuberculosis patients, where Leon was the radiologist, my memories become more numerous and more coherent. By this time I was six years old and was better able to understand what was happening to and around me. The hospital was located in a clearing in a large forest. How I loved those woods -- mostly because for the first time, I had some freedom to roam, away from Eda's watchful eye.

Compared to my barren years in the cellar, this forest and the adjacent meadow offered a wealth of treasures to explore. I gathered the first violets (those wild wood violets had a perfume unlike any violets I have ever smelled since) and brought a little bouquet to my mother as a harbinger of spring. I picked mushrooms and feasted on wild blueberries and raspberries. I played with the insects on the woodland floor. I went for walks on the paths, listening to the birds and watching the scurrying little creatures. I made daisy chains and clover wreaths and investigated every flower and plant. This knowledge proved to be useful many years later: during the summers between my years in college, I worked as a social hostess and children's counselor in a resort hotel in upstate New York. When I took groups of children for hikes in the wooded and mountainous areas, I was able to entertain the kids for long periods of time -- even the little ones -- by showing them which plants made a pop when you broke them on the back of your hand, which ones rattled, which ones made dyes, which ones could be used like miniature saws, how the backs of fern fronds were spotted with spores, how to whistle through a blade of grass, and many other plant tricks.

As a child, I spent most of my waking hours when we lived in the hospital playing in those woods and the meadow that lay in front of them. I even tried to plant a little garden, though I didn't leave enough roots on the plants I stuck into little holes I dug. I only watered them once or twice with a glass of water that I brought from our room, and they didn't get enough sun, so not surprisingly, they all died. But I am certain that this is where I learned to love nature, a love affair that has persisted throughout my life and one that I passed on to my husband, a Brooklyn boy who didn't know a tree from a daisy when I met him.

This was also where I met my first "boyfriend," Peter. He was the son of one of the doctors who worked with my father at the sanatorium. We would ramble through the woods together, and I taught him about all the plants and creatures that I had discovered. As I look at a photograph of us, taken by one of my parents' friends, I can understand why everyone thought we were "adorable" together. Peter, blond with what is considered typical Aryan features, is wearing leather shorts (*Lederhosen*) with suspenders and a vest over a short-sleeved white shirt. I have a white apron over my dirndl dress and the ever-present big white bow in my short dark hair. It must have been torture for Eda to keep her mouth shut when she saw us together.

Our apartment in the T.B. hospital in Gauting was small but quite comfortable. There were two bedrooms, so I even had a tiny room of my own for the first time in my life. I recall that we had a little balcony, which was the scene of another one of my near-fatal indiscretions. First, I need to fill in some background.

It was here in the small town of Gauting, a suburb of Munich (Gauting-bei-München) that I got to know Eda's surviving brother, Milek (Samuel). It turned out that Milek had been in charge of another DP camp in Ulm at the same time that we were interned in ours, but Eda and Milek had lost touch with each other and neither knew whether the other one was still alive and if so, where the other one was. Somehow they reestablished contact and found out that, while we were headed for America because Leon's skill as a physician made him a valuable asset, as an engineer Milek was unable to get a visa, so he was emigrating to Australia.

Our paths crossed in Gauting, and he stayed with us for a couple of weeks. He and I had to share my bed, and he complained every morning that I had kicked him all night long. He had a wonderful sense of humor. We'd be waiting at the train station and he'd cry excitedly, "The train, the train!" and when, filled with impatience, I asked eagerly, "Where?" he'd answer, "It's not coming!" I fell for it every time, and everyone would get a good laugh at my expense. It doesn't sound so funny now, but at the time, I thought he was the wittiest man alive (my sentiments about him were confirmed when my husband and I visited our Australian family many, many years later, not long before Milek passed away; he made us feel very welcome and kept us both smiling with his warmth and humor).

During the time we lived in Gauting, on many nights I heard a volley of distant but distinct pops. When I asked about it, I was told that it was hunters shooting deer or rabbits. One night when Milek and I were about to go to sleep, I asked him what those noises were, and for the first time I was told the truth: it was Germans who had rounded up trucks full of Jews and were shooting them at the edge of the forest. Sometimes in the early evening I would see those big army trucks covered with green canvas passing by and, from time to time, I would catch a glimpse of a face through an opening. I think those were the Jews who were headed for execution. People have said to me, "But this was AFTER the war!" Sometimes we are very naive in our thinking. In the silence after the war about the atrocities perpetrated during the war, there was a sort of tacit impression -- especially in this country -- that once the war ended, the Germans (and the Poles, who also hated Jews, as attested by the many pogroms) started to treat the remaining Jews with respect and dignity. Nothing could be further from the truth. The humiliation suffered by the Germans and the Poles upon losing the war was seen as tangible proof that they had been right all along, that the "dirty Jews" were the ones who were bringing misery to their people. Even after the war, the Germans and the Poles still hated the Jews, all the more so because in their minds, the Jews had caused them to go to war, had caused them to lose the war, and thus the Jews were the ones who were now bringing censure and shame upon their people. Hitler had convinced the Germans that the Jews were responsible for every evil, unfair, intolerable thing that happened to them and that therefore the Jews deserved to be scorned, tortured, and exterminated. Can anyone really believe that simply because the Allied armed forces defeated the armies of Hitler and his allies, the Germans suddenly had a change of heart and started thinking of the Jews as brothers? Long after World War II was over, hatred for Jews thrived in Germany and in Poland. Even today, there is no shortage of skinheads and neo-Nazis and Holocaust deniers. For the most part, they operate under the radar because today it is not a popular viewpoint. But in Hitler's Germany, any show of sympathy for the Jews was considered treasonous and punishable by death. Such depth of feeling does not cease just because a defeated nation signs a treaty to bring the war to an end.

So now, having set the stage and explained how the Germans felt about Jews, I can get back to telling you about my devilish deed. Because we had a German name (Zwilling, which means "twin" in German) and because none of us looked particularly Jewish, we were able to "pass." The doctors in the hospital didn't know that Leon was Jewish or, if they did, they were willing to look the other way because my father was such a skilled physician and his services were so valuable. Eda always loved to entertain and show off her skills as a hostess. She felt that as a doctor's wife, it was her duty to impress her husband's colleagues (and to bask in his reflected glory). One warm spring day, she was entertaining a few of Leon's colleagues from the hospital, who were seated on the little balcony. She asked me to carry some beverages out to the guests. I remember putting them on the table and turning to go back inside through the glass door. Suddenly possessed by a mischievous streak, I started singing "Bei mir bist du shoen" in Yiddish. I have never known Eda to react so quickly; hardly had the first couple of notes left my mouth when she flew across the room, eyes blazing, and clamped her hand over my mouth! Here was another time when I carelessly put all our lives in grave danger, but by now I understood that what I was doing was very bad, though a child of six does not fully comprehend what could happen. I was just bored and wanted to create a little excitement. Luckily for us, either the German doctors did not hear me (I had my back to them and was inside the door when I started singing softly) or they chose to ignore what they heard because my father was such an excellent doctor (the hospital administrators even sent him to courses in other countries so that he could come back and teach the new procedures to the rest of the staff; I have a priceless black-and-white photograph of him during one of these teaching sessions). Once again, our lives had been spared -- no thanks to me.

I'd like to digress for a moment to explain my theory of what possessed me to do things that I knew would get me in trouble and why children often disobey their parents, even when they are aware of unpleasant consequences. I believe that all our actions are determined to some degree by two opposing drives: the quest for adventure and the need for security. The need for security inspires us to put money into retirement accounts, to install fire and burglar alarms in our homes, to buckle our seat belts and obey traffic laws, to avoid anything that could make us sick or cause injury. The desire for adventure, on the other hand, is what leads people to explore caves, to climb Mount Everest, to parachute from skyscrapers, to engage in extreme sports, and to participate in activities that have some element of danger and/or excitement. Children can't go off to bungee jump or sail across the ocean or partake in any of the thrilling adventures that are available for adults. So they get their adrenaline rush by acting out, by doing those things that they know are forbidden and will bring some sort of punishment down upon them. The lure of the forbidden is irresistible for children and often for adults as well.

Case in point: many years later, when I was a student at the University of Michigan, a very strict alcohol ban was in effect. Any female student caught with alcohol, especially if she was under the legal age of 21, was summarily expelled. We came up with all kinds of creative ways to consume alcohol without being caught: we injected vodka into watermelons or oranges and smuggled them into the football stadium, we rolled up whiskey bottles in the rugs at fraternity dances, we dispensed spiked coffee from the coffee urns at parties. My best subterfuge was to go to the apartment of one of my boyfriends and make Jell-o using half water and half bourbon (I think today they're called "Jell-o shots," but in the 50s they were unknown). You couldn't tell by looking at this Jell-o or by smelling it, so I would carry a bowl of it into the dorm on many evenings, and it was funny to see a bunch of girls sitting around eating Jell-o and getting high. When I went to graduate school at Yale, I found myself in the elevator with the house mother one day. I asked her whether it was OK to keep beer in the little refrigerators on our floor, and her answer was, "You're a big girl now." At that point, all the excitement and adventure went out of drinking alcohol, and I decided that I really didn't like the taste and anyway, I'd rather eat my calories.

As children and young adults starting to make our way in the world, our desire for adventure and exploration often outweighs our need for security and comfort, so we frequently do the very things we were warned against: we touch the hot stove, climb the tall tree, jump off the barn roof, run out into the street. As we get older, we become increasingly aware of our mortality, and so our need for security starts to outweigh our desire for that thrill of discovery or conquest. In different people, one of the two drives is more pronounced than the other one during their entire lifetime. That is why some people, from the time they are quite young, are "nest builders" and tend not to venture far from home; they are grounded in practicality. Others, even in their 80s and 90s, jump out of airplanes, ride motorcycles, or ski on dangerous slopes; they are the dreamers, the explorers.

Comfortable as was our little walk-up apartment in the hospital, my parents were afraid that I would contract tuberculosis from such continual close exposure to the infected patients. So when they met a German artist named Paul Hey and asked him to rent us a room in his house, he agreed to do so. It was a large, farmhouse-style, two-story house. The ground floor was occupied by a family with four children. Mr. Hey and his wife lived on the second floor, where he had a studio in which he painted. They were willing to let us live in a large room on the second floor. The floor of the room was covered with an olive green linoleum, worn in many spots. There was a fireplace at one end of the room, opposite the door. My parents' bed was by the window, which had an outside fire escape. They placed a large beige folding screen down the middle of the room to separate my bed from theirs, giving them a little privacy. The bathroom, which we shared with the Heys, was a couple of doors down the hall, but there was a small washstand in one corner of our room. Compared to what I was accustomed to, this was real luxury.

Since heat was scarce and wood was plentiful, we often built a fire in the fireplace. One day my parents were taking me to a grownup affair, which they considered to be really important. Eda dressed me with great care in my one good dress, blue with tiny pale pink flowers on it, and combed my hair, carefully tying a big white bow on the top of my head. (To digress for a moment, I have seen a number of photos of little Jewish refugees, and they all have the same big white bow on top of their heads. The thought has crossed my mind that little Jewish boys can be identified by their circumcisions, and little Jewish girls can be identified by their pageboy haircuts with big white bows on top of their heads.) So here I am, all spiffed up, waiting for my parents to come back from an errand and to take me on this outing. Growing bored and restless, I noticed that the fireplace was full of burned-out bits of wood and quite dirty, so I decided to be helpful. By the time Eda and Leon returned, I was covered from head to toe with soot and ashes, as was most of the room around the fireplace. I have an indelible memory of the scolding I received that day.

As I mentioned before, I was a terribly picky eater. At her wits' end, Eda came up with a clever ruse. She would make a salad with grated carrots, grated apples, raisins, a little lemon juice, and brown sugar -- all healthy ingredients that would provide me with much-needed vitamins and minerals. It was not until years later that I found out that Eda used to prepare the salad and take it next door so that I would eat something nourishing. Since we lived in one room, she had to wait until I was asleep, then quietly grate the fruit and vegetables and take the salad next door. Mrs. Hey would invite me in from time to time, and I would come back home, raving about the delicious salad Mrs. Hey had served me (when Eda had tried to feed me the same salad some time earlier, I wouldn't touch it!). I never noticed my mother's expression when I would tell her about this wonderful treat that our neighbor had given me. With Mrs. Hey's kind cooperation, Eda got me to eat quite a number of nourishing foods that I would never eat at home. Mrs. Hey also had a trick that always fascinated me. She would say, "I am going to look at the ceiling and then I will tell you everything you had for breakfast." She would then roll her eyes toward the ceiling and proceed to intone, "I see soft-boiled eggs, strawberry jam, and milk." I could never figure out how she did that, completely unaware that I was wearing my breakfast all over my face and my clothes.

There was one food that I would eat without any coaxing. Espaliered on the side of the house was a peach tree. You could just reach out of the window and pick the biggest, juiciest, warmest, sun-ripened peaches I have ever seen. I still remember the way it felt to bite into one of those tender peaches, with the warm sweet juice running down your chin. Definitely no coaxing required. And there was yet another favorite: Eda made a delectable dish of sautéed mushroom and onions in a sour cream sauce. How I loved that dish! I would devour my portion of those mushrooms in record time, then I would ask Dad if I could "borrow" some of his. He would always ask me when I would pay him back, and I would always reply, playfully, "After the war" (meaning "never").

The Heys were very kind to us in a number of ways. Every Christmas they would invite us over and give us a few little presents. I was the star of the show, invited to sing all three stanzas of *Stille Nacht* (*Silent Night*), all of which I remember to this day. In Germany, instead of carolers, it was traditional for young people to come around dressed up in costumes (St. Nick, the devil, and other characters) and wish everyone a merry Christmas. I was terrified of these costumed characters. In a panic, I couldn't stop screaming, even when they took off their masks and revealed themselves to be older children whom I knew. I have no idea why they scared me so, but I still feel a twinge of the old panic when I think about those carnival figures.

There was another Christmas custom: if you had been good, St. Nick and his elves would leave you presents, but if you had been bad, the devil would leave you a willow rod or a lump of coal. Every Christmas morning I woke up with keen anticipation. The first thing that would catch my eye would be a willow twig tied with a red ribbon, resting accusingly on my pillow. Of course, I knew that I had been naughty, so I resigned myself to not getting any presents. Then I would slide my foot into a slipper by the side of my bed, and there would be something in the toe of the slipper. And here and there I would find little presents all day long. My parents couldn't afford big, expensive presents, but they always made sure I had a few little surprises to make my holiday an exciting one.

The family who lived downstairs, the Schmid-Burghs, had four children: Johann, Vroni, Peter, and Steffi. The youngest and closest to my age was Steffi, and she became my friend -- or at least, we played together. Friendship was an alien concept to me and was not part of my repertoire. It is difficult for people who have lived a normal life and who take relationships for granted to understand how foreign some of these concepts are to someone who has never experienced them. For instance, when Bob and I were married, we sort of eloped (that's a long story) and had invited only the closest family members: our parents, Bob's mother (his father had remarried, so I had two mothers-in-law for several years -- that's another long story!), Bob's brother and sister-in-law. When we returned from our weekend honeymoon, it was made clear to me that his family was displeased because we had not invited Bob's grandparents. How could I ever make them understand that the idea of grandparents never even entered my mind, since I had never known or heard about mine and did not understand the nature of that relationship? Of course I would have invited them -- if I had been aware of their existence.

Though the children in the house in Gauting tolerated me, especially the two younger ones, they often hurt me with their cruelty, which was sometimes unintentional, at other times deliberate. They often made disparaging remarks about Jews, about foreigners, about poor people, about the way I dressed and talked (I had learned to express myself in German while we were in the DP camp in Austria, but my German was certainly not of native fluency). One poignant example comes to mind. White flour was a scarce commodity at the time, and few people could afford white bread. Usually we ate the dark, thick peasant bread. One day, as Steffi and I were playing outside, her mother called her to come in. Turning to me, Steffi said, "We're going to eat white bread with butter and jam, but you can't have any." I know it's not unusual for children that age to be insensitive and mean at times, but this exclusion (when I needed so desperately to have some sense of belonging), this flaunting of superiority, this affirmation of the difference between us made a psychic wound that still throbs when I probe it with my tongue of consciousness.

Then again, I also did my share of damage. There was the time when the children got a doll carriage and a doll. This was the first real doll I had ever seen, and it filled me with amazement because it would open and close its blue china eyes and when you tilted it forward, it cried, "Mama." Was there ever anything more astounding in this world? Doll and carriage were left outside unattended one day. Drawn to it irresistibly, I lifted the doll out of the carriage and made it go through its paces a few times. I wanted to see how those magical eyes worked and, alas, I must have poked them a little too hard because suddenly they popped inside the doll. I tried my best to make them go back where they belonged but was not able to do so. I was much too frightened to tell anyone what I had done, so I tucked the doll back into the carriage and pulled the blanket up over her face, hoping against hope that by some miracle everything would be all right. I went inside and cowered in our room, waiting for the lightning to strike. I must have repressed the outcome because I honestly don't remember how things turned out.

Some time later the kids received a bicycle, all blue and shiny. One of the older children (I think it was the older boy, Johann) let me get on it while he held on to the back and let me pedal for a few feet. What joy! Then one day I saw the bicycle lying outside with no one around. I picked it up and, balancing on one foot, I put the other foot on the pedal -- just to get the feel of it. The temptation was too great. I found myself depressing the pedal and placing the other foot on the other pedal and my seat on the bike seat. Without meaning to, I found myself riding down the path. The back yard of the house had a sort of island of trees, surrounded by a wide semicircular gravel path. I was doing fine on the straight part and was starting to feel confident and to enjoy the feeling of locomotion. Then came the curve, and I didn't make it. Over I went, with the bicycle crashing down on me. Ignoring the pain in my knees and elbow, I disentangled myself and picked up the bicycle. But when I tried to push it back to where I had found it, I couldn't get the wheels to turn. The rim of the wheel had been dented in such a way that it was hitting the rear wheel, keeping it from turning. With great difficulty I half carried, half dragged the injured bike back and leaned it against the house. I was too scared to confess what I had done, and for several days I lived in torment, hoping for a miracle: maybe the siblings would blame each other and my crime would never be discovered. Predictably, their parents confronted mine, and some arrangement was worked out between them so that my parents would pay off the cost of the bike in installments. I don't remember what my punishment was, but I do know that Eda never forgot and forgave this incident -- she mentioned it not long ago as an example of what a difficult child I was.

The German elementary school was approximately two miles from our house. Children attended school either from 8:00 a.m. to noon or from 1:00 to 5:00 p.m. on alternate weeks. Because it was such a long distance and because we often had to walk in the dark, I was given special permission to skip kindergarten (which was in session during different hours) so that I could attend first grade with Steffi and walk with her. To describe the discipline in the school as strict is to understate the truth by at least half. The children were expected to sit absolutely still, eyes front, hands folded on their desks for hours on end. If you fidgeted or if your attention wandered, whap! the ruler came down hard on your knuckles. Your full concentration had to be on the teacher at all times because everything was taught orally and you had to be prepared to respond with lightning speed if you were called upon. All math calculations were done in your head and had to be performed with rapid-fire precision. For me, this was pure torture; I can still feel the sting of my raw knuckles when I think about it. That's probably why math is so difficult for me to this day. The only redeeming grace was that the teacher liked my handwriting, so I was frequently the one who got to write on the blackboard. While this eased the pain of having to sit still in my seat, it presented a whole new set of torments. For one thing, it exposed me to the constant malevolent scrutiny of my fellow students, always an uncomfortable situation, especially since my parents couldn't afford nice clothes for me. Also, it was very hard for me to write beautifully and still keep up with the teacher's pace; listening intently and writing at the same time was a real challenge for me. And if I made a mistake -- you guessed it: whap! Excruciating embarrassment in front of the entire class, not to speak of the physical pain. So I lived in a continual state of ambivalence, both hoping to be called to the blackboard and dreading it.

There was no such thing as recess -- such frivolity had no place in the serious business of learning. We must have had bathroom breaks, though I don't recollect how that worked. Did we learn the material? Yes indeed; the price of not keeping up with the class was too high. As a matter of fact, when we arrived in New York, I was so far ahead of my American contemporaries that, without knowing a word of English, I started out in the fourth grade but was quickly promoted into the second half of the fifth grade, ahead of my age group.

Even though my German teacher was a rigorous taskmaster who wielded her ruler with cruelty, she was not heartless or without compassion. One morning Steffi and I had a late start. As we began to run down the long, steep hill, I tripped and fell and slid all the rest of the way on my face and hands. By the time I reached the bottom, I was one scraped-up, bloody mess. There was no question of turning back, so I trudged on beside Steffi, crying all the way. The teacher took one look at me, rushed me into the bathroom, and gently tried to wash off as much of the debris as she could. When we got back to the classroom, she gave me a picture she had on her desk. It was an outdoor scene printed on a special paper so that when it was dry and sunny, the clouds in the picture were pink, but when it was rainy, they turned blue. I was so completely captivated by this bit of magic that I forgot all about my poor face and was able to sit through the whole morning of classes and to walk back home.

Eda became hysterical when she saw me, and my father was summoned at once. The debridement was an acutely painful process because I had large amounts of mud, pebbles, and shards of all kinds lodged in the wounds on my face and hands. Throughout, I kept looking at my wondrous picture, a gift from the woman who, until that day, had only given me whacks with the ruler. My father then determined that I needed a tetanus shot. Scared out of my mind, I grabbed his tie and kept pulling. To my horrified fascination, Leon's face turned from pink to red to purple, but I hung on to that tie with all my terrified strength. Gasping for air, he was finally able to dislodge my stranglehold in time to recover his breath. He didn't even rebuke me because he felt so sorry for my pain and fear, but I was smitten by terrible guilt about what I had done to my poor, kind father.

In spite of the difficult circumstances of our lives during the post-war years, there were moments of levity and laughter. The Polish expression for "good night" is "dobranoc." In a moment of silliness, we twisted the expression around into nonsense syllables, and this became our special saying when we were in a good mood. As I went to bed, if I said "nocibracala" (pronounced something like "notzibratzalla") and my parents responded with "bracinocala," I knew all was well in my little world, and I went to sleep with a smile on my face.

There was no public transportation to speak of and, of course, we couldn't afford a car, so we didn't travel much. I do remember that once we took the train to Munich and walked around the streets. At that time, Munich was a bombed-out city, the streets filled with the rubble of the many buildings that had been leveled to the ground. I had the opportunity to see Munich a few years ago, and I cannot believe what a beautiful city it is, completely rebuilt. When my husband and I visited Munich, we took the train to Gauting and tried to find the house where I had lived. We had gotten the address from a kind person in the Chamber of Commerce, who looked up Paul Hey's residence for us. On the corner of the street, next door to where I had lived, there was an American army base at that time. The Army base and Paul Hey's home are gone now, converted to an apartment complex. The street has been renamed to *Paul Hey Strasse*, a tribute to the painter who lived there (there is also a Paul-Hey-*Hauptschule* listed under "schools"). Many of the original houses on adjoining streets were still standing just as they had been -- pale yellow or light tan stucco with tile roofs; some had colorful murals painted on the walls. We didn't make it all the way down the hill to where my school had been because we got distracted by the sound of a young girl and some children speaking English; it turns out that there is a large English language school located nearby.

One more note about Paul Hey: at the time we lived in his house, he was beginning to acquire some renown in Germany. With great kindness, he presented us with several postcards and a small painting, on which he wrote little tributes addressed to my parents (*Den lieben Zwillingen zur Errinerung an Gauting und Heys* ["To the dear Zwillings as a souvenir of Gauting and the Heys"]). They were delighted to receive these samples of his work as remembrances of the few good things that happened to us in Germany, but I was distressed by the fact that he had written on the post cards and "spoiled" them so that we couldn't send them to anyone.

Today they are museum mounted and hang proudly on the walls of my dining room.

Two and one-half years passed in this way, and then I was told that we were leaving for America. Once again we packed our meager belongings in a couple of suitcases and set off for new adventures, with no idea of what lay ahead for us.

Coming to America

The Voyage

Before we left Germany and my Uncle Milek, he gave me a blank journal in which I was to record my adventures. On the flyleaf is a watercolor picture of a young woman in a red coat and a sailor hat with a ribbon streaming in the wind, standing on the deck of a ship with skyscrapers in the background, gazing longingly into her future. On the front page he wrote an inscription in German: "Think of us sometimes, even if you are far away from us." The inscription is dated 8 July 1949. I didn't use this book to record my adventures, but I have always treasured it, and it is one of the few possessions from that era that I still have. When we were leaving Germany, I asked our neighbors and my parents' friends to sign it for me. And when I graduated from high school, my classmates and teachers wrote their humorous, trite, or poignant messages of farewell in this journal. I take it out from time to time to read all the inscriptions, which bring back so many memories of people whose paths once crossed mine.

In September 1949, we boarded the American Navy troop ship, *General C. C. Ballou* (which spent nearly two years making the crossing between Europe and the United States carrying refugees) to cross the Atlantic. I remember clearly being packed into steerage with so many bodies -- men, women, children, youngsters, oldsters -- all huddled into a space designed to hold only a fraction of their number. Sanitation facilities were distressingly inadequate, as were sleeping and breathing space. Since we sailed at the height of the hurricane season in the Atlantic, it was a long, rough crossing. Not everyone was a good sailor, and many became violently ill. I absolutely could not stand the filth, the stink, the crowding. In desperation, I sneaked out onto the deck and hid behind one of the life boats. A sailor found me there and brought me before the captain. Trembling with fear, I told him that I would simply die if I had to stay in that miserable steerage compartment. This kind man took pity on me and allowed me to stay up on deck during the days, and the sailors even brought me lemons to suck on, which helped ameliorate the seasickness. I don't know how else I could have survived this nightmarish voyage.

To make matters worse, the two staples of our meals were eggs -- sunny side up and very runny -- and fish -- smelly, oily, greasy fried fish. It was many years before I could get myself to eat a fried egg, and I insisted that my eggs be cooked hard, long before the salmonella scare warned the general public that undercooked eggs could cause illness. I think it was at this time that I developed an allergy to fish. Every time I tried to eat fish, my stomach would revolt.

This condition once led to a bizarre experience. On a bus tour through Brittany with a group of French people in 1962 (when I was 22 years old), I was tempted by the beautiful preparations of fresh fish served in every restaurant. I told myself that the allergy business was all in my head, and I enjoyed a lovely fish dish for dinner. Around 3:00 am, I woke up suddenly with the urge to vomit. I knew that the WC was somewhere down the hall, but I didn't know exactly which door it was, and the hallway was very dimly lit. So there I was, stumbling down the corridor, blindly opening doors at random and evoking shrieks from the occupants, trying with all my might to hold back my sickness and praying that the next door would be the right one. This scenario convinced me that I would no longer select fish from the menu. I still get queasy when I smell "fishy" fish, and I can't tolerate the oily ones, but if it's very fresh, I can eat mild white fish without any unpleasant repercussions.

The hideous voyage culminated in one of the most awe-inspiring moments of my life. We were allowed to come up on deck as we sailed into New York harbor. It was still pre-dawn, and the buildings, the streets, and the memorials were all lit up. Ahhh, those lights! How can I possibly impart to you the magnificence of that sight? The only lights I had ever seen up to that point were the feeble street lights and the sparse lights in the modest homes around us, usually dimmed by curtains. I had never seen a skyscraper nor had I ever imagined that a building could reach up into the sky. I was so dazzled by this display of lights of every color as far as the eye could see that it literally took my breath away. I'm not sure whether we actually passed by the Statue of Liberty at that time or whether I'm confusing it with a later trip around Manhattan, but my impression is that we did sail past this wondrous monument, and it was so thrilling that I could barely contain myself! My life has been enriched by many happy moments, but nothing ever hit me with such explosive, overwhelming force as those lights. I must have developed a case of brain freeze because I remember nothing after that. Eda told me that thanks to our relatives and the Physicians' Committee, there was a taxi waiting on the dock to take us to our first hotel, so we didn't get processed through Ellis Island like most of the other refugees.

Let me digress here for a moment. When people hear the word "refugees," the picture that comes to mind is of a mass of dirty, unkempt, helpless, frightened figures, dressed in ragged clothes, most of whom can't speak English and are unable to communicate with anyone but each other. How do you think you would look if all your possessions were taken away, you had to live without your bathroom with all its amenities, without laundry facilities, without shopping malls, without your dry cleaner, your hair dresser, and all the people who work to make you look good, and if you were thrown into a country where no one spoke English and you didn't understand a word anyone was saying? But we clean up good, we refugees. Every roster of outstanding figures in any field of endeavor -- sports, entertainment, finance, government, industry, academia, literature -- is replete with the names of people who came into this country as refugees.

And so began another phase in my life.

New York, New York

We arrived in this country without any visible means of support. Although Leon was a well established physician in Europe, he didn't have a license to practice medicine in the U.S. He needed to pass his Board exam, but since he didn't speak English, he had to learn the language before he could even attempt to take the licensing examination. During the two years he spent studying and preparing for the examinations, we needed a place to live and a means of subsistence. This support was provided by HIAS (Hebrew Immigrant Aid Society) which, according to its web site, "was instrumental in evacuating the displaced persons camps and aiding in the resettlement of some 150,000 people in 330 U.S. communities, as well as Canada, Australia and South America." Leon also received a loan from his Uncle David (the one who had issued us an affidavit of support guaranteeing that we would not become public charges, so that we were able to obtain visas to come to this country); eventually he paid back every penny of this loan.

We were sheltered in a series of hotels in uptown Manhattan, in an area known as Washington Heights. Periodically, we were shunted from one seedy hotel to another. It was not an ideal situation but, as the saying goes, beggars can't be choosers. Because of the high population density in New York City, every time you move a couple of blocks, you go into a different school district. This change would have been pretty traumatic even for a "regular" nine-year old, but it was many times worse for one who was anything but "regular." For one thing, Eda dressed me in my one good, dirndl-style dress and brown high-top shoes with white lace socks; I also had a big white bow on top of my head. Needless to say, I didn't look like the other children on the block. To make matters worse, I didn't know a single word of English when we arrived in New York City. The first words I learned to say were "I don't understand." Have you ever noticed that people think they can make you understand what they're saying by talking more loudly? There I was, a scared little girl with no idea of what was expected of me, and people on the street were yelling at me in gibberish. Small wonder that I worked very hard and learned some basic English phrases in record time.

Going to school was always a struggle because I didn't know how to interact with the other students and the teachers. Every move to another school brought the agony of a new barrage of derision. In an age group where the worst insult you can hurl at someone is that she is "different," I was beyond different. My clothes were different, my hair style was different, my accent was different, and I was unbelievably dumb and ignorant because not only didn't I talk like the others, I didn't know anything about movie stars or music or even manners or any of the little things that *everyone* knows. Children that age can be very cruel, and I certainly felt my share of that cruelty. They taunted me mercilessly, and at times they even shoved me. I didn't have a clue as to how to fight back. Never in my life have I hit anyone in anger -- it's just not in me. And since I didn't have the verbal facility to defend myself, I left myself wide open to their attacks. By the time my classmates in one school got bored with the sport of making my life miserable, I was moved into a different school, and the torment started all over again.

There was another respect in which I differed from Americans my age. I had been raised in a culture where the pronoun "I" was written in lower case, while the pronoun "you" was capitalized, showing a mindset in which more respect was granted to the person addressed than to self. Moreover, in all the languages I had learned, there was a respectful form for "you" as well as a familiar form. The familiar form was used only in speaking to family members or close friends; everyone else was addressed with the respectful form. Young people, especially, were expected to show deference for their elders. It was a constant struggle for me to figure out various circumlocutions so that I would not have to address adults with the familiar "you," which felt offensively aggressive to me. One day, when one of my father's friends came to visit us, he told me, "Ellen, it doesn't matter how well you learn to speak English or how Americanized you become. Unless you learn to look adults in the eye when you speak to them, you will always be a stranger in America." It took a great deal of willpower for me to resist the impulse to keep my eyes downcast when I was addressing my elders, especially professional people who, according to my upbringing, deserved special esteem, but with time, I became "Americanized" in this regard.

When the father of a friend died, we were able to move into his small, rent-controlled apartment in one of those non-descript, multi-story, red-brick buildings featuring an ugly external fire escape. Clearly, architectural aesthetics were not a prime consideration in this neighborhood. I remember that the address was 54 Audubon Avenue, and the Google map tells me that it was located one block east of Broadway, between 167th and 168th Streets. Here we had a living room and a bedroom. There was a small dining nook with a table and three chairs in front of the window; the tiny kitchen alcove held a sink and a small oven/stove top (microwaves were not generally in use yet). The other side of the living room contained a sofa, a lamp, and a coffee table. At night I slept on the sofa, but during the day, Eda usually lay on the sofa, nursing a headache -- at least that's how I remember her (I learned to be more sympathetic and compassionate when I myself started suffering from migraines).

In fact, this sofa was the scene of a very distressing episode for me. Eda and I fought constantly. I hated having to play quietly in that cramped space while Leon studied, often with a colleague and friend who was in the same situation, having come from Germany at the same time we did (I believe her name was Kara Rosenkranz). I wanted to be free to play outside and explore the streets. But Uncle David's wife, Aunt Genia, conscientiously sent Eda every newspaper clipping of every kidnapping and every crime perpetrated against every child in the entire state of New York. Understandably, Eda was afraid to let me roam at will, especially since the neighborhood was not a very safe one.

On this particular occasion, Eda and I had had a real knock-down, drag-out, with lots of screaming on both our parts. Leon had been out running some errands. Upon his return, he found Eda in her "dying swan" position on the sofa, with a cold cloth pressed to her forehead. When she complained to Leon about what an impossible child I was, he turned to me and said in an accusing tone, "Look what you've done to your mother!" Rarely have I ever been so devastated! My beloved father, my hero, had turned on me and was blaming me for causing something that was a daily occurrence in our household: Eda always had a headache, with or without my insolence. And Leon never took sides; he just listened and made appropriate sympathetic sounds. I was so bewildered by his treachery and so angry at Eda for having turned him against me that I ran out of the apartment and walked the streets and didn't come back until after dark. Let them worry about me, it served them right! As I recall, I didn't even get punished for this insubordination, probably because both my parents were so relieved to have me home safe.

Part of the reason Eda and I were always at odds is that she resented me for tying her down and I, sensing that resentment, felt a strong sense of guilt, which aroused feelings of hostility toward her. Much later, when I was a grownup, Eda told me that she really wanted to take some classes to learn English and maybe get a job to help out financially during this period, but she wasn't able to do so because of me. Both my parents had instructed me repeatedly never to open the door to anyone when I was alone in the apartment. When one of Leon's friends knocked on the door one day and told me he wanted to come in and wait for Leon, I recognized his voice and let him in. This proved to Eda that I could not be trusted to be left alone while she attended classes. There were other occasions when I failed to follow instructions. One day, there was a leak in the refrigerator. Eda had to go out, so she left me a note not to open the refrigerator door. I came home with a friend and took some snacks out of the refrigerator. When Eda scolded me for disobeying her written instructions, my response was, "Next time, don't scribble."

My last in a series of schools was P.S.169 Manhattan, located on the corner of Amsterdam Avenue and 169th Street, a block and a half from our apartment building. The best thing about this school was that we all wore uniforms. The girls were required to dress in white middy blouses with red ties and pleated navy skirts. At least now I didn't stand out from the other youngsters so much, though I was still pretty ignorant about most of the things that came naturally to those who had grown up with American culture, and I still bore the brunt of a lot of ridicule. I had finished the third grade in Germany and was placed in the fourth grade when I started school in New York. Even though I didn't speak English at first, based on my overall performance, at the end of the first semester I was skipped into the second half of the fifth grade, ahead of my age group. When I finished the sixth grade, I was one of only a half dozen out of hundreds of students who passed the "rapid test," which would have allowed me to complete the seventh and eighth grades in one year and move into high school a year earlier. At Eda's insistence, I was not allowed to take advantage of this opportunity. No amount of arguing, crying, and threatening to run away from home was effective in changing my parents' decision. I was so angry at them that I hardly said a word to either of them for a month. I vowed that I would never forgive them, but I realized how wise they had been when I was in high school and all my classmates started wearing makeup, dating, and driving -- but I was too young. The same thing happened in college -- I was not old enough to drink (legally) until the second half of my senior year.

Little by little, I started to interact with the other youngsters in my class, and eventually I hung out with two girls in particular. One lived in the same apartment building as I did, on a lower floor. Her name was Eva Singer. Eva was also Jewish, and I get a kick out of her inscription in my journal. The little jingle normally goes:

Ellen is a good girl,
She goes to church on Sunday.
She prays to God to give her strength
To kiss the boys on Monday.

Eva had altered it to *She goes to school on Friday*, and she had changed *Sunday* to *Saturday*, sacrificing the rhyme, but keeping it religiously neutral. Eva's mother was divorced (a veritably scandalous state of affairs at the time), and since she had to work, Eva was almost always left alone in her apartment after school (a latch-key kid). Eva's mother was a smoker, and she left packs of cigarettes lying around where Eva could easily get her hands on them. She would sneak a handful of cigarettes out, and a few of us girls would go behind the school and light up. We thought we were just too sophisticated for words! My guilty conscience got the better of me, and one day I told my Dad about our smoking sessions, expecting him to be angry and to punish me. But Leon knew just how to deal with me. All he said was, "Well, if that's what you want to do, then it's your own health you're ruining. But do me a favor and don't tell your mother about it. She would get very upset." Suddenly all the glamour of sneaking the forbidden cigarettes was gone, and I didn't touch another one until I was in college.

The other third of the "terrible threesome" was a girl named Mary Hanley, one of a large family of Irish Catholics who lived a couple of blocks away. Mary's inscription in my journal is rather revealing of her belief system:

When you get married
And have 48,
Don't call it a family,
Call it a state.

Obviously, Planned Parenthood was not a strong tenet of her upbringing. The three of us spent countless hours roller skating around our neighborhoods, and we knew every crack in the sidewalks within a radius of some ten blocks. Our roller skates in those days were very different from the inline blades of today. They consisted of metal wheels attached to a metal frame that slipped around the bottom of your shoe. The frames were adjusted and tightened to fit with a metal key. That was the inspiration for the song *I've got a brand new pair of roller skates, You've got a brand new key,* which was popular when I was growing up. We didn't wear helmets or knee pads or any protective gear. If you fell down, which happened to me often because I am a big-time klutz, you went home with scrapes on your knees and/or hands or a bloody nose. Somehow we survived.

Another favorite activity was movies on Saturday mornings. For a quarter, you could spend most of the day in an air conditioned theater (none of us had the luxury of air conditioning in our apartments). You'd start out with a few full-length cartoons, then you'd have the news reels, and then there would be a double feature. If you got lucky, you might even get a live piano player or some other entertainer on the stage. You could easily spend five hours in the movie theater, giving parents a real break, since the movies were considered a safe place for young people to go by themselves; however, crossing Broadway was pretty risky business. Of course, we didn't have TV or computers for entertainment in those days.

Not all the times I spent with Eva and Mary were so much fun and so pleasant. Because I was such an easy target, they sometimes treated me harshly. One painful memory is a day when we were playing at Mary's house. I don't remember how the incident started, but I do remember that the two of them grabbed me and stripped off all my clothes. Then they tied my hands and feet to the wooden posts at the foot of Mary's bed. Several of Mary's siblings, with whom she shared the bedroom, came in and gawked at me, jeering, "Look at the Christ child!" When Eva and Mary finally untied me and let me put my clothes back on, I slunk home like a whipped puppy, head down and tail between my legs. The rage and humiliation that filled me that day didn't keep me from seeking out their company the very next day, so great was my need for acceptance and companionship. For several reasons, I never told either of my parents about any of these distressing incidents. I was too ashamed, an emotion that victims often feel. I was also scared that somehow, in her habitual fashion, Eda would turn it all around to make it my fault: "You must have done or said something that made them think it was a good idea to do this to you." Most of all, I was afraid that I would be forbidden to play with Eva and Mary, leaving me all alone again. Even torture at their hands was preferable to crushing loneliness.

Something that I found novel and exciting in my new home was the food. When we arrived in the city, I was bedazzled by the produce displays in the local grocery stores. I had seen local produce from the farms in Germany, but it was either growing in the fields or on the trees, or it was in our kitchen, ready to be prepared for our meals. Here in New York there were stores and stands with artistic displays of such a variety of fruits and vegetables that it gave me pleasure just to look at them. Once, when a kindly shopkeeper saw me staring longingly, he let me sample a prune plum. I thought it was the best thing I had ever tasted in my life, and I wheedled Eda into buying three pounds of them, since they were quite inexpensive because they were in season. When we got back to the apartment, I gorged myself on all three pounds at once. It was impossible for anyone else to get into the bathroom for the next couple of days, and I learned my lesson about gluttony the hard way!

Eda and I rode the subways to go visit friends or do errands that were beyond walking distance. Sometimes she would treat me to lunch while we waited for the next train. There were snack stands in the underground areas where you waited for the trains, and my idea of culinary heaven was a hotdog from one of the vendors, a small bag of Fritos, and a Nedick's orange soda. No gourmet meal at one of New York's most exclusive restaurants has ever given a wealthy diner as much gustatory pleasure as this combination did for me.

Uncle David and Aunt Genia went to one of the Jewish hotels in the Catskills every summer. Eda thought it would be good for me to get away from the heat of the city and breathe some fresh country air, so she convinced them to let me come with them for a week during our first summer in New York. What I remember most is that in the back of the hotel, there was a dark, musty old barn that had been converted into a rudimentary video arcade, with a ping-pong table in the center of the floor. That was the favorite hangout for the help and the few young people who were dragged to this hotel by their relatives. Of course, I wanted to spend my time with them. Uncle David and Aunt Genia had other ideas: they wanted me to sit outside by the pool with them. It goes without saying that a ten-year old does *not* want to lounge around a pool with a bunch of senior citizens, listening to them complain about their latest aches and pains! After several days of dragging me out of that barn, only to have me sneak back in, I was deemed unmanageable and incorrigible, and I was shipped back to my displeased parents. I think Eda welcomed the break from having to deal with me, and she was exceedingly disappointed to have her little respite cut short.

The following summer I was sent to Camp Ranger on Silver Lake, a three-hour bus ride from the city. When I Google Camp Ranger, I find the following description in the 1993 reunion book: "Camp represented so very much to so many of us -- fellowship, athletic competition, sharing, caring, hope and love. For many it was a coming of age. It was our first real taste of life and a special freedom away on our own. Camp Ranger was most of all a time to be with old friends and to make new ones." Yes and no. There was a certain amount of bonding because we were all in the same boat. For many of us, it was our first time away from home, and we felt a mixture of exhilaration, angst, homesickness, and excitement. But, for the most part, here too I was an outsider. I was not good at badminton, I couldn't hit a baseball or pitch or run, so I was invariably the last one to get picked -- reluctantly -- for any team. I couldn't swim -- I was perennially in the minnow category so that even the kindergartners made fun of me. My marshmallow was invariably the one that fell off the stick into the campfire. Worst of all, I was incurably gullible and therefore an easy target for all sorts of pranks and practical jokes. There was only one time when a practical joke backfired on the jokers. The girls in my cabin had short-sheeted my bed -- a trick that consisted of folding the top sheet in half and tucking it in firmly so that when the camper got into the bed, she would not be able to straighten her legs and would have to undo and remake her bed. They were all watching me surreptitiously as I climbed into bed, expecting the usual cry of annoyance. But I had short legs and since it was cold, I tucked my legs in under me, so I didn't even notice that my bed had been short-sheeted. For once, I had gotten the upper hand, even if it was through a fluke.

There were some good memories from my camp experience. I was pretty good at arts and crafts, and I made innumerable boondoggle bracelets and key chains as well as looped pot holders for my parents. I was also chosen for a role in our camp play, a little operetta about gypsies. I took my part so seriously (I still remember several of the songs) that I alienated the other members of the cast, who just wanted to have fun. And I did learn how to paddle a canoe. My favorite memory is of a group of us girls taking a few canoes out at twilight, spreading out across the lake, and singing rounds from boat to boat. People would come out along the shore to hear our sweet voices, which carried especially well at that golden time of day. I believe that was the only time during my camp experience that I felt a true spirit of camaraderie and contentment. The gray and red badge that I so carefully pasted into my scrap book still evokes that beautiful memory for me. I didn't form any lasting friendships, and I didn't go back the following summer because in the meantime we had moved to Clinton, NY.

One evening Eda and Leon, along with several of their friends, took me to an off-Broadway theater. The play was *On the Town* starring Nancy Walker. It was a musical with music by Leonard Bernstein. Probably the most famous song from this musical is *New York, New York*: "New York, New York, it's a helluva town: the Bronx is up but the Battery's down." I was enraptured. That night, I was sure that I was destined to become a famous actress and star in musicals. The fact that I couldn't sing or dance or even face an audience was not going to deter me. I pored over all the movie magazines I could get my hands on, and I clipped pictures of the glamorous stars. Eva Gardner and Cyd Charisse were my favorites, but June Allison was right up there near the top. When I decided to become a teacher, my dreams of stardom dissolved.

Two years went by. Leon passed his licensing exams, and we were ready to leave the city and to move to our next home.

The Clinton Years

Clinton, a village in upstate New York, needed another family doctor, and Leon accepted the position. Located in the Mohawk Valley between Utica and Syracuse, Clinton was -- and still is -- one of those sleepy little farming communities found throughout this sprawling country of ours. Its claim to fame is that it is the home of Hamilton College, "a highly selective, top-ranked, private liberal arts college... a national leader in teaching effective writing and persuasive speaking" (description from their web site). When we lived in Clinton, it was an all male college; it has since gone coed. The other main attraction was the skating arena, home to the Clinton Comets, a semi-professional hockey team. According to Wikipedia, "[t]he Clinton Comets were an American ice hockey team in Clinton, New York. Founded in 1927–28 as the Clinton Hockey Club and nicknamed the Comets in 1949, the team played primarily at the Clinton Arena from 1949 until 1973. From 1954 until 1973, the Comets participated in the Eastern Hockey League, dominating for ten of their nineteen seasons." Because Clinton is located in the snow belt of upstate New York and the winters are long and severe, life in this town revolved around the arena. Even before they could walk, toddlers were put on double-bladed skates and placed on the ice, where they soon learned to glide with grace. Small wonder that many superb hockey players and figure skaters, some of whom went on to star in national ice shows, were raised in Clinton.

I came late to the game, and I had neither athletic ability nor strong ankles. But Eda insisted that I had to learn to skate and, moreover, take part in the annual ice show. I practiced diligently and tried with all my might, but skating was a physically painful experience for me. My ankles never adjusted to the demands of ice skating, partially because Eda bought me skates a couple of sizes too big for me in the belief that my feet would grow into them (figure skates were expensive, and we couldn't afford to keep buying new ones.). My feet didn't grow, and the poorly fitting skates with wads of cotton stuffed into the toes didn't give my ankles proper support. The rehearsals for the ice shows and the performances themselves, in front of my classmates and their families, were agony for me. The first ice show in which I took part was *The Wizard of Oz.* I was the largest Munchkin ever seen and stood out with a humiliating lack of grace. The breaking point came when we did a show in which we were required to do an Irish jig on the points of our skates for what seemed like hours; I knew then that it was time to find another way. It would never occur to me to disobey Eda and quit the figure skating team, but I couldn't bear another year of pain and embarrassment. So the following year, every time Eda asked me whether I was in the show (she never came to rehearsals), I assured her that I was and that things were going well. Imagine her surprise when she came to the show and found out that I was in the control booth, doing Cinderella's voice! Technically, I hadn't lied to her -- I *was* in the show. At that point, she must have realized that figure skating was not in my future, and she never again forced me to participate in any athletic event.

Another of my mother's attempts to civilize me ended up as a complete fiasco. We were the only Jewish family in Clinton, so it goes without saying that there were no synagogues in town. When Eda decided that I needed to be educated on the subject of Judaism, I had to travel ten miles by bus to Utica to attend Sunday school. I hated and resisted being forced to attend these classes. Here again, since I got a late start, I was the oldest in a class of all boys. Every one of those boys would have preferred to be out playing with their friends, and I made a ready target for their annoyance at being coerced to sit in class on Sunday mornings. They would dunk my pony tail in the ink wells that were built into those old-fashioned desks, they would collapse my folding chair so that I landed on the floor, they would scatter my papers all over the floor when the teacher's back was turned, and they would even pinch me or hit me from behind. Because I was a girl and so much older, the teacher expected me to be mature and demure, but it seemed to her that I was always at the center of class disruptions. Finally it became too much for her to handle, and I was kicked out of class. I can't tell you what a relief that was to me! Not to have to stand out in the cold and snow early on Sunday mornings, waiting for the bus, was a welcome reprieve. I never felt I was learning anything useful in that class, so it was worth braving Eda's displeasure not to have to put up with those bratty boys every Sunday.

Many years later, when my mother-in-law expressed the opinion that our daughters really should know something about their Jewish heritage, we enrolled Lisa in Sunday school in Galveston. After a few weeks, we literally had to drag her in, fighting all the way. We learned that the boys in her class were doing mean things to her -- like putting ice cubes down her back -- because she was the only one who completed her homework and made them look bad by comparison. It was here she learned that doing homework was not "cool," and when she started slacking off in public school and her grades dropped as a consequence, we decided we had to pull her out of Sunday school. Sometimes history does repeat itself.

What are my religious beliefs after all that I've lived through? I think that if there were an omnipotent God, He would not be petty enough to demand that you worship in a specific place by reciting prescribed prayers in a certain order, or that you eat -- or refrain from eating -- certain foods during certain times. I respect people who derive comfort from practicing rituals that they believe help them achieve some degree of holiness, but for myself, I do not subscribe to organized religion of any ilk. How could all those prescriptions for worship have come from God when there are so many different formulae and when they change from time to time as groups splinter off from the precepts of their creed? And how is it that every group is convinced that they alone know the right way? I know it's not for me to question or to understand God's plan, but how can I believe in a benevolent God when I observe the inhuman cruelty that we humans perpetrate upon each other in the name of religion, especially when innocent children are made to suffer? I believe that no matter what religion you follow, there is only one commandment: strive in all you do to follow the Golden Rule. If you treat everyone with the kindness and respect and dignity that you would desire for yourself, then you are fulfilling the mission for which you were placed on this earth. As I quoted earlier from Henry Roth's *Mercy of a Rude Stream*: "A *mensch* is a *mensh*, *goy* or Jew," and I would add "or Muslim or Hindu or Catholic or Protestant or adherent of any other religion or sect."

Clinton was one of those towns (according to Census 2000, the population is 1,972, but I suspect that may include a few dogs, cats, cows, pigs, horses, and other assorted "family members") where everyone's grandmother had gone to kindergarten with everyone else's grandmother. Strangers were not warmly welcomed, and foreigners were objects of curiosity but were not embraced by the residents. Over time, Leon's skillful and compassionate ministering to the families -- and even to their animals in emergency situations -- won over the hearts and trust of the residents. For me, it was a different story. Once again, I was the "odd man out," only this time my differences stood out even more sharply in this homogenous community. We were the only Jewish family in town, so we did not go to church on Sundays. By now, my English was practically indistinguishable from that of a native speaker, but my parents spoke with a pronounced accent. I was still pretty ignorant about many of the "Americanisms" that my peers had heard in their homes from the time they were born. But the worst thing about my situation was my pathological shyness, which today would be labeled as "social anxiety disorder." Indeed, I suffered from anxiety attacks at the mere thought of having to interact with people. It was so bad that if I saw someone I knew approaching, I would cross the street just so that I wouldn't have to exchange greetings with that person. Since I had just come from "the big city," my reticence was mistaken by many for snobbishness -- that uppity kid who thinks she's better than us because she's used to city life.

My seventh-grade social studies teacher apparently shared this opinion, and she set out to teach me a lesson. It's not surprising that cataclysmic events -- earthquakes, tornadoes, fires, floods -- can have a devastating effect on people's lives. What *is* surprising is the way simple, seemingly innocuous things, like a three-word sentence, can also affect our lives in such a disastrous way. One day Mrs. Luther called me up to the blackboard to write the answer to one of her questions. As I walked down the isle in my brown high-top shoes, I was accompanied by a rather loud squeak with every step. As if this weren't embarrassing enough, Mrs. Luther said pointedly to the whole class, "Cheap shoes squeak." How I wished the ground would open up and swallow me right then and there! It still stings when I recall this episode. Just three little words, but this incident became for me one of those "enduring vulnerabilities" that John Gottman speaks of in his book *The Relationship Cure*.

Here again Leon knew just what to do. He had set up his practice in the front part of our house on College Street. He had hired a nurse to help him in the office and Eda took care of the bookkeeping, but I was the one responsible for sterilizing the instruments, emptying the ashtrays and wastebaskets, keeping the magazines in the waiting room tidy, and other small chores. I did all this when the office was closed, so I had minimal patient contact. When he became aware of how hard it was for me to interact with people, Leon placed me at a desk in the waiting room. Every day after school and during weekends, it was my job to greet patients as they came in the door, ask their names, and pull their charts out of the file. At first this seemed like the worst punishment he could have imposed on me, and I went through agony every time I had to speak to one of the patients. But as time went by, it became increasingly easier for me to greet the patients and even to chat with them while they were waiting for their appointments.

As my confidence in the waiting room built up, it became easier for me to interact with my peers, and I began developing some tentative friendships. It wasn't easy to be my friend because my excessive lack of self-esteem manifested itself in some deplorable ways. For example, every time the teacher handed back a test, I would go around asking, "What did you get? You only got an 84? Well, *I* got a 96!" It makes me blush to think about how obnoxious that sounded and, of course, none of my classmates understood that I was only trying to say, "See, I have something worthwhile to offer, so please like me. Just look how smart/clever/competent I am; I deserve your affection." Obviously that's not what my classmates heard, and instead of winning them over, I alienated them even further. I wanted so desperately to belong, to be noticed, to have someone care about me that I sometimes pulled some pretty dumb stunts. I remember one day when the snow was just melting and there were dirty patches of it all over the grass. A couple of my classmates had stopped at my house on their way home from school, and we were playing some kind of tag game in the back yard. As usual, I was losing badly, so when one of the girls tagged me a little roughly, I "fell" down. No one paid any attention to me, so I just lay there for a long time with my face in that dirty snow, feeling inordinately sorry for myself and angry at the other girls for ignoring me. For a long time afterwards, I felt guilty whenever I remembered this incident. I thought that lying still, freezing on the snowy ground was just a bid for sympathy, a way of calling attention to myself -- and there may be an element of truth in that. But when I learned about how cutters hurt themselves so that the physical pain blocks out emotional anguish that is too much to deal with, I realized that this was what I was doing. The emotional pain of not belonging when other children seemed so in tune with each other was too overwhelming for me to process at that point in time. Years later, when I was in counseling, I told my therapist about a similar incident when I "punished" my peers by refusing to go out with them and hunt for chocolate Easter eggs. I just stood at the window and watched them having fun. She asked me whether I liked chocolate Easter eggs, and I replied with an enthusiastic, "Oh yes, I love them!" Then she asked whether I got to eat any that day, and I sadly admitted that I didn't. Her next question was, "So who was the one being punished?" Light finally dawned, and I came to the realization that martyrdom doesn't pay; only the martyr winds up being hurt.

I remember very little about our small house at 37 College Street, except that it had a front porch with a couple of chairs on it. On nice evenings, after the dishes were done, neighbors would come out to sit on their front porches, and frequently they would come over to chat about the events of the day. I remember one such evening. I had gone for a walk and, as usual, I had stopped to pet all the dogs in the neighborhood. I longed to have a dog -- or any pet, for that matter -- but Eda had a fear of dogs, so she used the office as an excuse to deny my repeated requests (though in later years she learned to love my gentle Mugsy and my adorable Yorkies). On this particular evening, when I was returning home, I saw Eda sitting on our porch. As I approached, I saw a horrified expression taking shape on her face. What I didn't realize was that a whole parade of assorted dogs had followed me home. And to make matters worse, one of the big dogs -- a large lab, I think -- jumped into her lap and started covering her face with slobbery kisses. I thought she was going to pass out, but I was so doubled over with laughter that I wasn't able to help her. Finally my Dad heard her screams and came out to pull the dog off her. It must have been a whole week before she ventured out on the porch again.

My first "romantic" episode took place while we were living in this house. A classmate named Sandy had become my "best friend," and we often spent time at her house. Her father raised and trained horses, and her mother always made me feel welcome in their rambling farmhouse. Sandy had a date for the eighth-grade spring dance, so her date's friend, Irving, asked me to go with him. We spent an exciting week decorating the gym, and I was thrilled beyond words to be part of a group. We draped so many lilacs all over the gym that the smell was overpowering, and there was a great deal of sneezing that evening. I was -- and have always been and still am -- a terrible dancer; my brain knows what I'm supposed to do, but my feet simply will not follow, so I was not sorry when the dance ended. Then a wonderful thing happened: Irv walked me up to the door and planted a little kiss on my cheek. I was so flooded with emotion that I didn't get any sleep that night -- my hand kept straying to the spot where *a boy had kissed me!* The memory of that first kiss still brings a smile to my lips. Somehow I made it through seventh and eighth grades, and then I was a high school freshman at Clinton Central High. My graduating class had seventy-five students, which gives you some indication of the size of our town.

Eventually we moved from College Street to our home at 28 Fountain Street; in retrospect I always picture us in this house during my Clinton years. This was a two-story white farmhouse with a sizable backyard and a converted barn out back that served as our garage. For some reason, a scene out of *To Kill a Mockingbird* comes to mind whenever I think of this house. My husband claims that the square footage of the house is actually much larger than the living space because there were so many layers of wallpaper plastered on top of each other that the walls literally bulged outward! My father's office was on the ground floor, along with the large kitchen, a bathroom, and a tiny side room (I assume this was once a pantry, but my mother put a small bench in there and used it to take catnaps during the day); our living quarters were upstairs, consisting of two bedrooms, a bathroom, and a living room. I now had my very own room with a bed, a desk with a wall mirror, and a closet -- just like all the other girls. The room even had a window that looked out on the backyard. What I remember most about this room is the shiny pink quilted bedspread. I spent many hours either on top of that bedspread when it was hot or under it when it was cold. In bed was the safest place for me to be; I didn't get into constant trouble when I was in bed. On Saturday mornings I loved to stay in bed and listen to a whole series of radio programs for kids. My favorite was *Let's Pretend*; I learned a lot about Americana from the stories told by Big John and Sparky.

One of the other two doctors who treated the population of Clinton had a daughter, Buffy, who was in my class. We had an on-and-off friendship because I was still a difficult person to have as a friend. I was very eager to have schoolmates come to play at my house, but they hardly ever wanted to come over because we had to be very quiet, since Leon's practice was downstairs. The moment our play became a little boisterous and loud, Eda or Leon would come upstairs to shush us. My parents never had the time or the inclination to sit and chat with us or offer us snacks. My house was just not very inviting for teenagers. Buffy was known as a "brain" and I was a fellow "brain" -- she graduated as valedictorian and I was salutatorian of our class, with only a small fraction of a GPA point behind her. Today we would be labeled as "geeks,"

69

and so this common bond drew us together. Buffy and I got along pretty well, but several times, when she decided it was time for her to go home, I didn't want her to leave, so I would lock her into my room and refuse to give her the key. I feel such shame when I write this, and I knew it was wrong when I did it, but I couldn't help myself -- I was so afraid that she would never want to come back that it was my very behavior that pushed her away. This was a pattern I followed most of my life; after reading many books on behavior theory, I've been able to forgive myself because I now understand that my actions are not so strange considering my childhood. To use Gottman's terminology, I kept making bids for emotional connections, but I always did it the wrong way.

Even though memorization was easy for me and I learned quickly, I had to work harder for my good grades than my classmates because there was so much about art and literature and civics that was second nature to them but was a mystery to me. Beethoven, Balzac, and Botticelli were not exactly household words in our home. I didn't know about George Washington and the cherry tree, Motown, homilies, common expressions like "the elephant in the room" (I thought there literally *was* an elephant in the room!), colloquialisms, Monopoly and Bingo, brand names like Kleenex, quotes from the Bible, the *Farmers' Almanac*, the constellations, Twinkies, the names of common plants and animals, and a whole host of things that are almost innate knowledge for every American kid. For instance, I think it's safe to say that just about every American child is familiar with ice cream. The first time I was given ice cream, I had no idea what it was. I told Eda that it was very good but much too cold; I'd like it better if she warmed it up for me a little. I had so much to learn! My facility with languages didn't help me much in learning English because it is such a difficult language -- there are more exceptions to the rules than there are rules. For years I went around mispronouncing words that I had read because I didn't realize, for example, that the pronunciation of "destined" was different from "refined." And when it came to manners and etiquette, I was a complete clod. During our senior year of high school, one of my classmates asked me to be a bridesmaid in her wedding. I was thrilled that someone actually wanted me to play such an important part in her life. The rehearsal luncheon was held at the country club, and by watching carefully what the others did, I was able to use the wide array of utensils in the proper order. In the middle of the meal, we were served a scoop of sorbet in a glass dish. How was I supposed to know about cleansing your palate between courses? I had always been taught that sweets spoil your appetite, so I set mine aside for dessert. I was terribly disappointed when the waiter removed the dish and I never got to eat that delicious lemon sorbet; I was also so embarrassed when I realized what a gaffe I had made that I remember the incident to this day. My life was a minefield of such social traps, and my ignorance of American customs and mores frequently made me a laughingstock, thus further undermining what little self-confidence I was able to muster.

Eda was often in a grumpy mood because she was always busy and tired from cooking, cleaning, and mostly from managing the billing for my father's office. Leon was one of the last of the old-fashioned country doctors and family physicians. When one of the three doctors in town retired, a would-be replacement, after trying to fill the position for several days, departed with these words: "The people of Clinton don't want a doctor. They want someone who will go chasing all over the countryside at all hours of the day and night for hardly any pay!" He was right. Leon charged very little for office visits and not much more for house calls ($3 or $4), which often involved many miles of driving through the sprawling farmland. Even at those low prices, many of the farmers couldn't afford to pay him, and we were sometimes compensated in flowers, eggs, corn, or whatever the family had on hand. Unfortunately, the bank that held our mortgage was not keen on accepting chickens as a monthly payment, so we had to raise enough cash to pay our bills. This was a real challenge because the migrant workers who passed through town during the summers had no money, so Leon treated them free of charge.

I still recall an incident that is emblematic of my father's character. Around 3:00 one morning, someone leaned on our doorbell with great persistence. Thinking that there was an emergency, Leon put on his robe and slippers and rushed down the stairs. My window was open on that hot night, so I was able to hear the exchange that took place. The migrant worker at the door said, "Well, doc, I gots a col', but I kin come back in the mornin' ifn ya wants me to." With admirable restraint, my father answered, "Yes, please come back during office hours." As he climbed back up the stairs, I heard him mutter some unkind words under his breath, but like the true gentleman that he was, he never complained about the incident to anyone.

I mentioned that Leon made house calls during the night from time to time. Like many people (and animals), I have always been afraid of thunderstorms. For some reason, I had the impression that the only safe place during a thunderstorm is in a moving car -- I guess because that way the lightning can't catch you and the thunder is muffled by road noise. Anyway, Leon knew this, and whenever he would have to go out during a storm, he would come into my room to wake me, though I was usually awake and scared. I would slip on my raincoat over my pajamas, and he would let me ride with him while he made his call. Invariably, the housewife would invite me in, and I would sit in the kitchen eating cookies and drinking milk while Leon tended to the patient, and then we would head home again. I loved the cozy feeling of being warm and dry in the car with my Dad while the storm raged outside. This was often the only chance we had to talk, since we both had such busy schedules. Predictably, Eda was not happy with these outings and scolded Leon for keeping me from getting my sleep, but he just smiled and murmured some placating sounds.

Since our kitchen was on the ground floor, behind Leon's office, sometimes our meals had some interesting twists. One day, as I was eating lunch, I noticed that there was a glass jar on the other side of the table that had something strange in it. When I asked Dad what was in the jar, he simply said, "That's a spontaneous abortion" (I guess he meant miscarriage), as if that were the most natural thing to be sitting on one's kitchen table!

Occasionally our meal would be interrupted by a child with a cut or a wound that required debridement and a tetanus shot. Dad would call me in, and I would hold and talk to the child and try to distract him or her while Dad was cleaning the wound. When it was time for the shot, I would watch for my cue and then I would ask, "What color lollypop would you like?" By the time the child answered me, the shot would be all over and it would be too late to cry.

Since I seemed to have a knack for relating to children, I started taking on babysitting jobs when I turned thirteen -- at twenty-five cents an hour -- to earn a little pocket money. As the official doctor for Hamilton College, Leon had a patient whose wife gave birth to a son. They asked me to babysit for him one day, and with much apprehension about handling a newborn, I accepted the offer. I loved taking care of little Daniel, and the Lewises were so pleased with my services that I became their official babysitter. Since I didn't date, I was free on weekends, which was very convenient for them. I proved myself to be responsible and trustworthy, and they called me often; sometimes I even spent the night in their apartment if they came home very late. They knew they didn't have to worry that I would invite any of the college boys into their apartment or throw parties while they were away. I took care of Daniel until he was three, and it was hard for me to leave him when I went off to college. My decision to become a teacher grew out of my babysitting experiences. It turned out that I loved working with young people, so teaching seemed like a natural career choice for me.

The babysitting jobs were the first in a series of jobs I held during the summers of my high school years. At the end of my junior year, with a glowing recommendation from the Lewises, I got a job in the Recorder's Office of Hamilton College. I had to type military forms for students graduating from the college. This was long before computers and word processors and even electric typewriters. The forms had to be typed in seven copies, using carbon paper between the sheets. You had to line them up precisely or the print would not come out in the right place on the line. Then you had to pound the keys very hard so that the impression would come out legibly on the last couple of pages. And if you made a mistake, you had to use whiteout on all the copies and line them all up again with great care. It was a boring job, but I was happy to have some spending money, and I felt very grown-up working in a college office.

During the following three summers, I worked as a social hostess and children's counselor in a resort hotel in the Adirondacks, on Fourth Lake, near Old Forge. My parents had been going to that hotel for several years during the summers, so they knew the owners and convinced them to give me the job. I loved that job. During mealtimes, I worked in the office. After breakfast, I would check the work of the chambermaids to make sure the rooms were all made up properly, then I would take the young kids on hikes or mountain climbing or, if the weather was bad, I would entertain them indoors. I looked so much like a kid myself, with my pony tail and shorts, that often adults would ask the owners how they could let those children wander out unsupervised. After lunch, I organized a volleyball game or some other games for the adults. All the help had a little time off in the late afternoon, and we often went swimming together in the icy water. On rainy days, we would give the guests a laugh by wearing our raincoats out on the dock, then stripping them off and diving into the lake. After dinner, I would organize some sort of entertainment for the adults, like Las Vegas Night or hayrides or singing around a campfire. When all the chores were finished, the help would hitchhike into town to have a drink and dance at the local bar. Sometimes, when the bar closed down at 2:00 am, we would go down to the beach with the band members and party into the wee hours of the morning. But I could always be counted on to be at my desk in the office bright and early. How I maintained this schedule all summer is beyond me now. Ah youth! Sometimes the Beckers would go away on business for a couple of days and leave me in charge of the whole place. Mrs. Becker would always hand me a list of "to do's" and she would invariably tell me, "Ellen, I know you are perfectly capable of taking care of everything, but do me a favor and get a couple of little things wrong so that I'll feel needed when I come back." I was accustomed to being made to feel inadequate, and this faith in my ability was so novel that it gave me a heady sensation. During the summer after my senior year in college, I had a similar job in Lake Placid, which I also enjoyed greatly.

Before I get to those later years, I must tell you about one of those traumatic episodes that still fills me with embarrassment whenever I think of it. During my freshman year, I joined the glee club, since I had so little athletic ability and the glee club required no special talent. As the time drew close for our big holiday performance, all the girls were buzzing about the dresses and shoes they were going to wear. I prevailed upon Eda to splurge this one time, and she bought me black suede pumps with chunky heels and a lovely pink organdy strapless dress -- and pink cotton socks trimmed with lace to match. For once I was going to look as good as the other girls, and I felt proud and happy when I admired myself in the mirror. As we were primping in the girls' room before going on stage, I noticed that some of the girls were whispering and snickering and looking pointedly at my feet. It was then I realized that they were all wearing nylon stockings, and it suddenly struck me how inappropriate it was to be wearing ankle socks with heels. Had I not been so flustered and embarrassed, it might have occurred to me to take off the socks and just wear the heels on bare feet, which wouldn't have been so noticeable. But I was too mortified to think straight, and so I went out on that stage and sang with the rest of the choir, even though I wanted to turn around and run out of the auditorium, and I cringed inside every time I saw (or imagined that I saw) people in the audience staring at my feet and turning to whisper to their neighbors. Once again I was a laughingstock, an outsider, someone who didn't belong. I wish I had known enough at the time to point out that Dorothy wore socks with her ruby slippers in *The Wizard of Oz*, though I don't think that would have made much difference. On the ride home, when I tried to explain to Eda how terrible I felt being ridiculed by the other kids, she dismissed my feelings in her usual way, "It's not so terrible. They'll all forget about it by tomorrow morning." I cried myself to sleep that night under my pink bedspread.

There were many nights when I quietly cried myself to sleep, and not always because of mental anguish. Often I had a gnawing ache in the long bones of my legs, mostly in my thighs. It may have been a case of severe "growing pains," but I suspect that I also had some osteoarthritis due to the time I spent in that cold, damp basement during my years with the Polish family; sometimes that dull ache in my thighs, hips, and calves still kicks in when the weather turns cold and rainy. I also suffered from severe stomach cramps, often accompanied by embarrassing bloating and gas. On numerous evenings my silent evening prayer would conclude with, "God bless mother and Dad, and please, dear God, don't let my legs and my stomach hurt so much tomorrow." Yet I never told my parents about these pains. Eda always made me believe that there was a stigma attached to any physical weakness and that it was wrong to admit to such imperfections. I knew in advance that she would have told me to be brave and to think how lucky I was compared to people who had "real" problems. If I had a broken leg, Eda would say, "Look at that guy. He has *two* broken legs, so you shouldn't complain." I always thought to myself, "Yes, but my leg still hurts," though I knew better than to say this to her.

In 1963, I was working in New York city writing programmed instruction for The Diebold Group (as we all still called it, even though in 1954 it was incorporated as John Diebold and Associates, a management consulting firm specializing in computers and automation that "provided consulting services to dozens of large U.S. corporations representing a wide variety of industries, as well as government and other public entities." When I interviewed with Mr. Diebold, who coined the term "automation," his comment was, "She'll make an attractive addition to the office."). It was not until then that I finally decided I needed to get myself checked out because the abdominal pains were severe enough to frighten me. I asked my father to make an appointment for me with a gastroenterologist in the hospital in Utica, where he sometimes worked, and I drove home to get an upper GI Series, which revealed that I did indeed have a small duodenal ulcer. Even more poignantly than my emotions about the diagnosis, I remember that drive. It was the day of JFK's funeral, and as I listened to the radio account of the way his son saluted at his gravesite, I was sobbing so hard that I wasn't paying attention to where I was going. I missed the turnoff onto the Tappan Zee Bridge, and I was well into Connecticut before I realized my mistake. A long drive turned into a very long, sorrowful journey.

Eda was no "Soccer Mom" -- most of the time, she was too busy and too tired to drive me anywhere. I walked to and from school every day, and if I stayed late for glee club or archery or some other activity, I sometimes walked home late in the afternoon. I don't remember exactly how old I was when I decided that I wanted to take piano lessons. Eda thought this was a worthwhile pursuit, so she found a lady who gave lessons in her home, and I started my musical career. We couldn't afford a piano, so I trudged dutifully to my teacher's house several times a week and spent a few happy hours practicing my assignments. Finally I had found something that I enjoyed and was able to master with relative ease. My teacher said that in all her years of teaching, she had never had a student who advanced so quickly. Even though most of her students started at a much younger age, I practiced very hard and literally flew through the various grades. And then winter arrived, with the bitter cold, the deep snows, and the short days. It was not possible for me to get through my practice sessions and walk home before dark, so Eda put an end to my lessons. She claimed it was because she didn't want me walking home after dark, but I think it was because the lessons and the sheet music became too expensive. I protested and pouted mightily, and in a way, I was sorry to give up something that earned me uncommon praise, but part of me was relieved not to have to take that long walk and to push myself to excel. I knew I didn't have enough talent to ever become a really good player -- I would never be a concert pianist -- so I convinced myself that it was just as well I was quitting while I was ahead.

Playing the piano didn't require athletic prowess, which is why I was able to achieve some modicum of success in this endeavor. When it came to anything to do with athletics, I was a complete washout. I dreaded phys. ed. classes. We dressed in our short burgundy cotton gym suits and, rain or shine or snow, we ran up and down the field trying to hit the ball with our hockey sticks. I could neither run fast nor did I have the strength or skill to get the ball away from my opponents. The only saving grace was that I was often allowed to play the position of goalie, but that was no walk in the park either -- I generally came home with big bruises on my shins and even bigger ones on my ego. Indoor gymnastics were even worse. I just don't have the coordination to stand on my head or do a cartwheel, much less to do flips on the parallel or uneven bars. I even had a hard time getting up on those skinny bars, and keeping my balance once I was up there took every ounce of willpower I could muster. But I desperately wanted to have an athletic letter "C" to sew on my jacket, so I was happy when I discovered that I could sometimes hit the target in archery. Through many long hours of practice, I finally became good enough to participate in a sufficient number of archery tournaments to earn that coveted letter. As for dance classes, they presented me with an even greater challenge. Let's just say that if I were a celebrity and for some unfathomable reason I decided to go on *Dancing with the Stars*, I would not be the first to be eliminated from the competition; I would the first one to be eliminated unequivocally even *before* the competition started!

Athletics may not have been my forte, but linguistics were. French was my favorite subject, and I was very good at it. Apparently my tenth-grade teacher thought so too because when the men in the drama club at Hamilton College needed a girl to play the part of Lucinde in Molière's *Le Médecin Malgré Lui* (*The Doctor in Spite of Himself*), she recommended me for the part. I'm not sure why they needed a French major, since the part called for a mute girl, but I was more than a little proud and honored to be chosen. Rehearsals at the college with all those good-looking young men were certainly the highlight of my year. Then came the night of the performance, and I couldn't wait for my parents to see my big stage debut. I kept peeking out from behind the curtain, but their seats were empty. And they remained empty throughout the evening. As had happened so many times before, my father had to treat a last-minute emergency, and so my parents often were not there to see my performance/recital/award ceremony/speech. I was bitterly disappointed that there was no praise forthcoming from the two people whose approval meant more to me than the congratulations I received from so many others. Since Leon's office was in our house, he was on call 24/7. On those rare occasions when he got one of the other doctors to cover for him because we planned an outing or a vacation, we were never sure whether we would actually be able to get away. Countless times we would be backing out of our long driveway when a car would pull in at the front. Invariably, we would have to carry our suitcases back into the house and unpack, resigned to the fact that Leon would have to take care of a patient and perhaps accompany the patient to the hospital.

Whenever this happened, I vowed solemnly that I would never marry a doctor. So I married a man who was studying to become an electrical engineer. Then he went on to get a Ph.D. in bioengineering. Then, after a few years, he went back to school to get an M.D. and became an anesthesiologist. For a number of years, he was on call for liver transplants, which usually took place at some ungodly hour. I am convinced that the hospital tapped into our phone line so that whenever we had plans to go to the theater, a concert, or dinner with friends, the scheduling people would say, "Looks like Feinstein has some interesting plans for tonight. Let's call him in to do a liver." I can't tell you how many times we would have to leave in the middle of a performance or friends would have to take me home after dinner while my engineer-turned-doctor rushed to the hospital to administer the anesthetic for a liver transplant patient. Whenever I complained about this to Eda, she just chuckled.

In addition to his home-office practice, Leon was also on the staff of the hospital in Utica. Oddly, this was the main reason for our name change. When we arrived in Clinton, our name was Zwilling (pronounced *tsvilling*), which means "twin" in German. For some reason, this name was difficult for people to spell and pronounce. Today, when we seem to have no problem identifying famous people with names that are ethnic tongue twisters, it's hard to understand why this name was so problematic. But remember that we are talking about a time when movie stars had names like Doris Day, Peggy Lee, Rock Hudson. After the umpteenth time the loudspeaker paged some garbled version of his name and the mailman delivered a letter addressed to an unintelligible name, Leon decided that he'd had enough. At least, that's what I was told; I now suspect that Eda was the one who initiated the idea of changing our name so that it would be harder for the "authorities" to find us. She never got over her fear that someone from the past would hunt us down and we would all be deported for some mysterious "wrongdoings" during the war. Eda was also extremely sensitive to anti-Semitism, both overt and covert, so I think she would have felt more at ease with a "neutral" name.

At any rate, they sat me down with a Manhattan phone book, which we had brought with us, and assigned me the task of picking a new name. There were certain criteria imposed by the courts. For example, you couldn't pick a name that was very common, like "Smith" or "Jones." The name couldn't be too long and complicated -- something we didn't want anyway -- and it couldn't have the characteristics of a definite nationality. In addition, I wasn't supposed to pick a name that contained an "r" or a "w," since Eda and Leon had a hard time pronouncing these consonants (long after I left home, whenever I picked up the phone and heard "sveetharrrrt," I knew Eda was about to tell me something I didn't want to hear). My own criterion was that the name had to start with a letter near the beginning of the alphabet because I was tired of being last on every list and in the back row of every class. After much deliberation, we settled on "Benton," and we had our name changed officially.

No matter how Americanized and neutral my name was, I remained an outsider. I had an almost-twin. There was a girl in my class whose birthday was the same day as mine, though I was a year younger. Deanna and I decided to have a joint party, and we spent many delightful hours planning what we would wear, what refreshments we would serve, what music we would play, and what we would do for entertainment. As the date drew closer, I was filled with excitement and anticipation -- until I found out that Deanna planned to invite only couples to the party. I didn't have a boyfriend because Eda thought I was too young to date, and I was too shy --and too afraid of rejection -- to ask a boy to go to the party with me, so I wound up staying home alone, torturing myself with visions of all the fun my classmates were having at Deanna's party. The following Monday, those cruel fellow students, my supposed "friends," told me all about how I should have been there because they had such a good time.

Clinton had a movie theater (in those days, theaters only had a single screen) during the time I attended Clinton Central High. One afternoon I had gone to a movie with a couple of the girls. We had parted ways, and I was alone on the last part of my walk home. There was an empty field behind the Grange where some of the older boys used to hang out. As I was passing by, one of them called out to me. I walked over to where they were standing and sitting, and I have to admit that I started flirting a little. One of the guys reached out and grabbed me, and then all the guys were putting their hands on me, groping me and trying to kiss me. Terrified, I broke loose and ran the rest of the way home. I never told anyone what had happened to me because I was too ashamed. In spite of my fear and disgust, I couldn't help being turned on. Even though this was a relatively harmless incident, it helped me to understand how victims of sexual abuse must feel. I believe that the reason rape victims so often harbor feelings of shame -- even when they know that they are not to blame in any way for the attack -- is that our bodies betray us. Our minds are screaming out in horror and revulsion, but those treacherous hormones respond to the stimulation in their own way, and we become sexually aroused in spite of ourselves. This involuntary reaction causes so much shame and guilt that sexual violence often goes unreported.

I don't know how I would have gotten through those difficult years without Carolyn. She was the nurse my father hired to help him after his practice was established. Even though she was an adult and was entirely professional in the office, she was young enough to remember and understand the emotional roller coaster of those tormented teenage years. My situation was complicated by my relationship with Eda and by the fact that I had no siblings or close friends to talk to. Carolyn was a very patient and empathetic listener, and I always felt better when I was able to share my frustrations with her. She was the one who answered questions for me that most girls asked their mothers. Many years later, when I was in Seattle, I re-established contact with her, and we got together whenever possible. She moved away, but we still keep in touch through frequent emails.

I was not sorry when my high school years came to a close. I had my heart set on going to the University of Michigan, but even though I was accepted, I almost didn't get to attend the college of my choice. Eda had seen a magazine article showing couples kissing good-night on the porch of one of the dormitories just before curfew, and she thought this was so sinful that I should not be exposed to it. I managed to convince her that I would behave myself, and she finally gave in. She traveled to Ann Arbor with me a day before orientation so that I could become familiar with the campus. As much as I had wanted to get away from home, when the time came for Eda to leave, I panicked. I clung to her as she said good-bye, and she got into the cab, leaving me waving and crying forlornly in the rain, unaware that my life was about to take a dramatic turn for the better.

PART II - MOTHER AND I

Why I Am Who I Am

In her book *The Red Tent*, Anita Diamant says, "If you want to understand any woman you must first ask about her mother and then listen carefully... The more a daughter knows the details of her mother's life -- without flinching or whining -- the stronger the daughter." This quote made me realize that, fight it as I may, I am the product of my mother's upbringing. Gottman's research has revealed that "...a large part of a person's knack for emotional connection is... determined by what happens in the home." According to him, children who don't learn to connect with parents early on frequently have trouble reading their playmates' social cues and are perceived as too bossy or too shy. They're the outcasts of the playground. Gottman continues, "As they move into their middle-school and high-school years, these same children can find it difficult to unlock the unwritten codes of teenage social interactions. When it comes to the complex tasks of negotiating cliques, making and keeping friends, or getting a date, they may feel awkward or 'clueless.'" As I read these words, I felt as if he were talking about me. Throughout my school years, I watched with envy as other children formed friendships and cliques, seemingly without effort. I was always the outsider, the foreigner, the one who didn't belong. I would try anything I could think of to be noticed and included, going so far as to lie face down in the snow and pretend to be injured just to get a little attention and sympathy. Unknowingly, I was following my mother's precept that you win friends by impressing people with your superiority or by playing the sympathy card. Life has taught me that people like to associate with those who make them feel good.

Why did I think it was necessary to include a whole section on my relationship with Eda in what is essentially the story of my memories and my experiences as the result of the war? In *The Emperor of Ocean Park*, Stephen L. Carter writes: "And I must spend enough time remembering my mother that she, too, can finally take a proper place in the rooms of my memory. If memory is our contribution to history, then history is the sum of our memories. Like all families, mine has a history. I would like to remember it." Since I have no memories of my biological mother, other than the one scene I described at the beginning of this book, I would like to "spend time remembering" Eda. Her body may still be alive according to medical criteria, but her essence is now only a memory to me.

As for why my relationship with her is inextricably linked to the effects of the war, had it not been for the war, I might well be an entirely different person. An infant who is rocked, cuddled, touched, soothed learns a different form of communication than one whose cries are ignored. A toddler who is encouraged to take her first steps into her mother's waiting arms develops a sense of security that is missing for a child who never receives any encouragement. A child who is praised for her efforts and achievements grows up with a sense of self-worth that is lacking in one who receives only indifference or criticism. My chances to receive nurturing, encouragement, approval were shattered when the war wrenched me out of my parents' arms. By the time Eda came into my life -- or I came into hers -- I had already established many patterns of behavior. Nevertheless, more than anyone else I have encountered in my lifetime, Eda had a profound influence on the person I have become. The effects of war reach far beyond the battlefield in space and time. Those who survive bear scars -- sometimes physical, sometimes psychological, often both. Eda survived the war with her body intact, but her mental scars affected every aspect of her life for the subsequent sixty years. Her life was shaped and consumed by fear of anything beyond the narrow confines of the familiar. Consequently, my upbringing was shaped to a large degree by Eda's post-war world view.

From time to time, I have wondered how differently I would have turned out if not for the war. I doubt that my father would have been a good influence on me, since from everything I have heard, he was not a good person. But what would life with my mother have been like? Would she have cuddled me and made me feel loved and special? Would she have told me that I was a good child and I could grow up to accomplish anything I tried? Would I have felt secure, confident, trusting? Would my personality have been entirely different? I know that I would have been surrounded by aunts and uncles and cousins and grandparents, since my mother had four siblings. Would I have had brothers and/or sisters? Would I have stayed in Poland and led a life that was entirely different from my life here in America? Would I have been coerced into an arranged marriage? I will never know the answers to these questions. I only know what my life with Eda was like.

From the very beginning, our relationship had many unusual aspects. She didn't witness my babyhood, didn't nurture me as an infant, didn't see me take my first steps or hear me utter my first words. There was no bonding between us early on. You might point out that many children are adopted and that their mothers still cherish them as their own. The difference is that those mothers *wanted* a child. Eda did not; she only took me in because of a promise she had made to her sister, who was then killed in the war. I came into Eda's life at a critical, tumultuous period, and many sacrifices were required of her and Leon in order to care for me. Small wonder that she harbored resentment toward me in her heart of hearts and that I was never able to please her or to feel truly close and comfortable with her. Have you noticed that sometimes I have referred to Leon as "Dad" but that Eda is always either "Eda" or "mother"? I could not bring myself to call her "Mom," with all the informality and intimacy implied by this endearment. Eda tried her best to feel motherly love toward me, but all her "I love you's" were tinged with "How much easier my life would have been if you hadn't come into it." I never felt truly wanted, accepted, loved unconditionally. Throughout my life, I felt that I had to *earn* Eda's love, that she could -- and often did -- grant it or withdraw it at will. "... [U]npredictable parents hook you deepest with intermittent reinforcement," says Louise Erdrich in *The Painted Drum*. "[Y]ou become that rat who presses the lever a thousand times for a kind word, a gesture of love."

From my mother I learned that love is conditional upon my striving unceasingly to please her. If I succeeded, I might be rewarded with a smile and a pat on the cheek and a "you're a good girl." If I failed, as so often happened, I was punished by a withdrawal of all signs of acceptance and affection. Love had to be earned. Unconditional love was not a quadrant of my emotional universe until I had a husband and daughters of my own. Small wonder that I grew up to be a people pleaser. I went along with everything that was said, regardless of whether or not I agreed, because I had been taught that people do not like you if you argue with them. I would twist myself into a pretzel to accommodate anyone who asked something of me, no matter how inconvenient or burdensome the task might be, because I had received the message that people only like you for what you can do for them. I was the one who always tagged along for fear of being left out. Everything I did was designed to ingratiate myself to others in an effort to win the approval and affection I craved so desperately.

In 1975, when I was working as a research associate in medical education at the University of Texas Medical Branch, my boss sent me to a professional meeting in Chicago. Several of the attendees were making tentative plans to go to dinner, but since I didn't feel like taking a cab to an expensive restaurant (mostly because I hadn't brought any dressy clothes with me and I didn't want to look out of place), I decided to go to a nearby eatery. One by one, the others opted to join me. This simple turn of events marked a watershed moment for me. It was the first time that I actually followed my own direction and didn't end up alone. People actually *wanted* to be with me -- what an astounding revelation! I didn't have to tag along and beg to be included. It was possible for me to claim my preference without alienating those around me. This was the germination of a newfound confidence, a realization that I could express my convictions without losing my friends. At long last, the seeds of self-esteem had taken root. I now had the courage to become a leader, to disagree with people without offending them, to say "no" when I had a good reason for refusing to do something that was asked of me.

How can I describe Eda? She was a perplexing mix of strong-headed independence and child-like neediness. Perhaps the best way to portray her is through free word association. These are the descriptors that come to mind when I think of Eda: petite, attractive, elegant (her favorite word), charming, gregarious, childlike, and vain. Also astute, generous, well-meaning, highly principled, proud, and vain. Eda could also be obstinate, judgmental, opinionated, domineering, self-indulgent, egocentric, manipulative, impatient, and vain. But she was also easily offended, prone to worry, insecure, fearful, and -- you guessed it: vain

Eda was a poster child for vanity. When I say she was terminally vain, I mean it literally. It was her vanity that made her worst nightmare become reality. After my father's Alzheimer's disease got to the point that she could no longer care for him and had to put him in a nursing home, driving to visit him became problematic for her. Let me backtrack a little. Early on the morning of Monday, April 9, 1984, I got a hysterical phone call from Eda. Not only was Leon behaving in ever more bizarre ways, but her sweet, gentle husband was screaming at her, accusing her of stealing from him and of hiding things from him. Since not much was known about Alzheimer's at the time, she was completely clueless about why he was acting this way and she was terribly distraught. I called my boss at work to say that I would not be coming in, phoned the airline and made a reservation on the next plane to New York City, called a friend to take me to the airport, called our cousins in Long Island and asked them to pick me up when I arrived, threw some clothes into a suitcase, barricaded the dog into the kitchen, wrote a note for my family to explain where I was going, and left the house within an hour of Eda's call.

Our cousins, Dorothy and Manny, were at the airport to meet my plane and drove me to my parents' house in Kingston. They stayed through dinner and tried to help me to calm mother down and explain to her what was happening to Dad. The following day I went to Dad's doctor with Eda to discuss the situation. According to the arrangements made with the doctor, the Public Health Nurse came on the next day to evaluate Dad's condition and the home situation. I took mother grocery shopping and tried to help her get as many things in order as possible to make it safe for both of them and to have help readily available in case of need. The following day I took a limousine to the airport and flew home to my family. I located a copy of *The 36-Hour Day* and I sent it to Eda by overnight express. She told me later that it did help her to understand what was happening.

I have to give Eda a great deal of admiring credit for how hard she worked and how many sacrifices she made to care for Leon at home for as long as she could. She is a little lady and he was a big man, so it could not have been easy for her to change him and clean him and support him physically. In the fall of 1985, it finally became too much of a burden for this 76-year old woman, and she made arrangements for Leon to go into a nursing home. By no means did this solve all her problems. The home was some distance from Eda's apartment, and the winters in Kingston are long and hard, with several feet of snow on the ground for most of the winter season. Eda's apartment didn't have a garage -- she kept her car in a carport. Whenever it snowed, she had to find someone to clear the snow off her car and to shovel the drive around the car. And it was difficult for her to drive in the ice and snow to visit my father. When she had an "argument" with a bus during a late storm in the spring of 1986, I put my foot down and told her that she absolutely *had* to move into a senior living center in St. Louis, where I could be close by to help out. It took some doing, but I finally convinced her that she could live independently in an apartment while Dad lived nearby in a nursing home.

So, in mid-May of 1986, Eda came to town and we started making the rounds of all the nursing homes/senior centers in the area. Not only was it impossible to find something that pleased her, the big problem was that nursing home beds were so scarce that they could only be held for a few days. Eda needed several months to wrap up all her affairs in Kingston and to get ready for the move. At last, we found that Delmar Garden Villas of Chesterfield -- which was quite new and attractive and was staffed by kind, attentive people -- was in the process of building an Alzheimer's wing and therefore they could guarantee the availability of a bed for my father and an apartment for my mother in six months.

Now came the task of measuring the rooms and making the rounds of the furniture stores to select furniture for her bedroom and living room. We also went to a couple of banks to open accounts and rent a safe deposit box, to the local grocery stores so that mother could familiarize herself with them, to several local restaurants, etc. All this while I was holding down a job as well as running a household with a husband who was frequently on call and so needed special attention, two daughters home from school for the summer who also needed special attention, a dog and a cat that needed my attention as well, and -- most time-consuming and stressful of all -- we were in the process of having a house built, and to say that things were not going smoothly would be the understatement of the century. My stress meter was off the charts because I was torn between the demands Eda was making on my time and energy with her frequent telephone calls asking me to take care of things for her; the headaches we were encountering with contractors, electricians, plumbers, roofers, painters, bricklayers, and the swarm of workmen involved in our construction project; the time and effort required to perform my job satisfactorily; and my family's complaints that I was not paying enough attention to their needs.

My journal entry for August 22, 1986, reads: "ADT came to fix alarm, Ehrlich installed new cook top, new washing machine arrived. Took Genette [Ami's friend from Galveston who had been spending a few days with us] to airport. Parents arrived -- got them settled." What the journal doesn't say is that we had moved into our new house just a week earlier, and everything that could have gone wrong did go wrong -- and then some! Yet when Eda and Leon arrived at the airport, Lisa and I were waiting at the gate with an attendant and a gurney on which Leon was wheeled into the waiting ambulance. All the arrangements had been made so that Leon's transition into the nursing home went seamlessly. When Eda entered her apartment, the furniture was set up and in place, all the utilities and the telephone were turned on, the TV (which we had bought for her) was on a stand and in working order, the refrigerator was stocked with all the foods she liked, there was a basket of fruit and a bouquet of flowers on the table -- everything had been done to make her new home attractive and comfortable. I didn't expect expressions of gratitude, but neither did I expect to be berated furiously because I had written "Alzheimer's Disease" in the diagnosis line of the registration form. After all, the only reason that a bed in the nursing home was available for my father at Eda's convenience was that he belonged in the new Alzheimer's wing. But that bit of reality didn't register in Eda's mind. She was determined that everyone should believe he suffered from Parkinson's because a physical illness bore less of a stigma than a mental one. In spite of all my efforts, hardly a visit went by in the ensuing years during which Eda didn't point out to me how lucky the other residents were because their daughters/sons/nieces/nephews did so much for them while she always had to struggle to do everything herself. Also, she did not tell the owners of the nursing home or any of the people with whom she associated that she had a daughter who lived nearby. I guess she felt that she could play the sympathy card more effectively if people thought she was all alone than if they knew that she had a daughter who helped her with everything.

Since her apartment was across the driveway from the nursing home, she was able to walk over to visit Leon without any difficulty. It was a comfort to me to have her in that senior apartment because over her bed was a button that she could push to summon help. But being Eda, she insisted that she would never call for help because they would then call the ambulance and everyone at the Villas would know that there was something wrong with Eda (in other words, that she was not perfect). She lived up to this vow, and several times I had to rush over because she called to tell me that she had fallen and cut her head or sustained some other injury. She never broke any bones, so she never had to go to the hospital, and none of the residents found out that her body was imperfect -- like the bodies of her mortal neighbors.

The culmination of this fear of showing any weakness came on July 19, 2001. I was spending the summer months in Seattle to escape the heat and humidity of a St. Louis summer. Only two weeks earlier, I had come back to St. Louis and my daughter Lisa, whose birthday is on July 3rd, had also come to commemorate Eda's birthday (she always used to say that since her birthday was on July 4th, she had come to the right country because here everyone celebrated her birthday with fireworks). We had a lovely three-day celebration, which Eda seemed to enjoy immensely. At one point, she said, "I've outlived all my relatives and friends. I'm ready to join Lonek [her pet name for my father]. I just want to go to sleep and not wake up." She said it matter-of-factly, and it didn't sound morose or self-pitying. Alas, her wish was not to be granted.

On July 19th, I got a call from Eda's friends. Apparently she had gone to the grocery store and to exercise class that morning. One of the staff members noticed that when Eda came out of class, she was walking erratically, clinging to the wall. After a conference with the director, over Eda's vehement protests, they decided to put her in a taxi with instructions to take her to the doctor, who was located in a hospital only a couple of miles away. Upon examining Eda, the doctor recommended strongly that she be checked into the hospital for observation. But Eda would have none of it and insisted that she would be fine once she got home and rested a little. Unable to make any headway against her obstinacy, he called the friends whose number she had listed as emergency contacts. They came to pick her up and take her home, then they called me in Seattle to tell me that Eda's speech was somewhat slurred and she appeared to be weak and dizzy. I asked them to put her on the phone and told her, "You are going to the hospital. NOW! No arguing!" (as she started to protest).

She finally agreed to go, but she refused adamantly to let them call an ambulance because she didn't want the other residents to see her being escorted out by the paramedics; she wouldn't even allow them to use a wheel chair because the other residents would "talk." (Vanity, thy name is Eda!) So Jean and her husband propped her up between them and managed to get her back into their car and drove her to the hospital. In the meantime, I made frantic phone calls to the doctor to apprise him of the situation. Sadly, by the time Eda got back to the hospital and was checked in and seen by the doctor, the three-hour window for successful tPA (tissue plasminogen activator) treatment -- which might have improved her chances for recovering from the stroke -- had passed.

I rushed back to St. Louis on the next plane, but by the time I arrived, there was not much I could do, except sit by her bedside day and night so that they wouldn't have to put her in restraints because otherwise she would keep pulling out her nasogastric tube. Her massive stroke left her paralyzed on her right side. Despite all my efforts to get her into aggressive rehab, she never regained the use of the right side of her body, and her deterioration -- both physical and mental -- has continued for almost seven years.

This vain and fastidious woman -- who went so far as to make arrangements at a funeral home some distance away because she didn't want people she knew to see her naked, even after she had died -- now had to submit to the indignity of being changed and bathed and dressed by strangers. While she was still able to communicate with some lucidity, she used to beg me to give her something so she could die; of course, I couldn't do that, though it broke my heart to see her suffering. Even though she now weighs sixty pounds and has been in hospice care for almost two years, her survival instinct is so strong that it will not allow her to let go and to find peace. In the meantime, I will always live with a double dose of guilt: because I couldn't help her to end her suffering when she asked me for lethal medication, and because I broke my promise to her that I would never put her in a nursing home. My reasonable mind knows that I had no choice. Small as she is, she is a dead weight and there is no way I could have lifted her and changed her and cleaned her. I didn't have the facilities to care for her. I couldn't stay home with her all day, every day because I had to go to work. The real decisive factor was that my husband would not have tolerated my bringing her into our house and spending all my time and energy caring for her. All these reasons make sense. But my emotional heart can't banish the guilt for not being able to help my mother after she did so much for me. I'll just have to live with it...

Let me give you another example of how Eda's vanity manifested itself: she was obsessed and distressed by wrinkles. When our daughter Ami was going through the pains of divorce proceedings, Eda's advice to her was: "Try not to worry, darling. You'll get wrinkles." As I read the advice one of Isabel Allende's characters gives in *Daughter of Fortune*, "... do not make faces because that causes wrinkles," I could easily hear my mother's voice saying those words to me. From the time I was in high school, when she was in her forties, Eda would deflect every compliment and kind word with something like, "Why would anyone want to talk to me or look at me when I have so many wrinkles?" Since I was an avid sun worshiper my entire life, my face started to show the ravages of tanning without benefit of sunscreen when I turned forty. That was when Eda launched her campaign to convince me to get a facelift. Her mantra was: "You have to get plastic surgery early because if you wait too long, it won't work as well." Given a choice, I would rather have a smooth face and a youthful appearance. However, I am not overly bothered by wrinkles. I think they are a reflection of the emotions one has experienced during one's lifetime. This attitude infuriated Eda and caused her to rev up the intensity of her cause with unremitting fervor. In this context, my (step)mother-in-law Rose did me a great disservice. She once told Eda that if you wish to bend someone to your will, the best way is not to confront them directly but to "inject" your thoughts into their heads subtly and repeatedly. Eda embraced this concept with annoying enthusiasm.

Not that she needed coaching in the art of oblique innuendo over the direct approach; she had mastered this technique long before Rose came along. With a posture becoming an admiral, she marched through life, determined to bend everyone to her will -- not by being forthrightly assertive but simply by wearing down her protagonist. Her idea of tact was to couch her criticisms in oblique references. For example, one day she thought that I was driving too close to a school bus in front of us. Rather than saying, "I wish you wouldn't follow that bus so closely," she launched into a story about a friend of hers who was driving too close to a school bus and got stopped by a policeman who gave her an expensive ticket. Eda's prescription for diplomacy and tact: never say what you mean directly. Use homilies and hints, analogies and anecdotes, metaphors and similes -- anything to disguise your message. I never understood the purpose of these oblique innuendos. If you got the point she was trying to make, what was the advantage of having to work for it? And if you didn't understand what she was trying to tell you, the whole ploy was senseless anyway. But I guess Eda felt that if she didn't voice a direct criticism, then she could always deny an ulterior motive to her story and she wouldn't have to take responsibility for her remarks.

Eda was relentless in her crusade for me to get my wrinkles smoothed out surgically. Seldom in all the years I can remember did she show any interest in how I felt, the quality of my life, whether I was happy. If I volunteered information about back pain or other ailments, she dismissed my complaints with annoyance, implying that I had brought these on myself by doing too much. Even if she knew that I had been sick with a bad cold or a migraine, she didn't ask whether I felt better. Every telephone conversation began with "How do you look?" Her only concern, on which she harped incessantly, was the fact that my face (and later my neck) had wrinkles. She never missed an opportunity to predict that my friends would desert me and my husband would leave me for a woman who didn't have ugly wrinkles. As a matter of fact, the threat that my husband would leave me was trotted out every time I did something of which she did not approve.

Shortly after we finished building our house, I took a two-week trip to Italy with a woman friend. Afraid as always of my leaving her alone for any length of time, Eda tried to dissuade me from going by saying, "You've worked so hard to build and furnish this house. How would you like to come back and find Bob living in it with another woman?" According to her, the only way for me to reverse this aging process was to give up all the activities I enjoyed (like gardening, volunteer work, activity groups, social events, travel) and to sit at home and get lots of rest and thus "take care of myself." Her idea of love was to call me first thing in the morning to tell me that I looked more wrinkled than any eighty-year old she knew. No matter how good I felt when I started out in the morning, after a phone call from Eda, I had to engage in big-time attitude adjustment to counter the effects her negativity had on me. Once, when I was still in my early forties, she called to ask me what brand of moisturizer I used. Flattered that she would seek my advice, I readily told her the name of the brand. Her reply was, "I only asked because you are so wrinkled that it obviously doesn't work and I wanted to make sure I don't use the same one." Squelch! When she was in her sixties, Eda had a facelift. A few years later, my father's Alzheimer's disease began to manifest itself, so she was preoccupied with his care.

At age eighty-nine, when she was living in the senior residence, she decided to get another facelift. We were all upset, knowing that the immune system is compromised at that age and that she was therefore vulnerable to a higher risk of infection, poor healing, and other possible complications. Why take such a risk in her situation, when a facelift would not have improved the quality of her life in the least? Her granddaughter Lisa even called the doctor's office and begged him to refuse to do the surgery. (I would have called, but I was afraid that Eda would find out and turn her full wrath on me.) But no amount of pleading, reasoning, threatening, or cajoling could deter Eda from her resolution to try to regain her youth. Unbeknownst to me, she had already made an appointment and put down a sizable deposit for the surgery. It was only through the fortuitous coincidence that I had surgery at that same time to release a painful trigger finger that this possible risk to her wellbeing was averted. Because my incision took an excessively long time to heal enough so that the stitches could be removed, she became frightened and backed out of the procedure.

She was convinced that the reason the surgeon agreed to refund her deposit was that he had fallen in love with her. She would often tell me, with a shy little smile, how he treated her with special consideration and devoted more time and attention to her than to any of his other patients. She even went so far as to find his address in the telephone book and to ask one of the staff members to drive her past his home. I didn't have the heart to point out that she was old enough to be his mother, although I doubt that this observation would have made a difference anyway.

In March 2001, she had a small TIA and went to her doctor. I had asked her to call me as soon as the van brought her back to her apartment, and I immediately asked her what the doctor said. Her reply: "He was so worried and so concerned about me. I felt bad because he took so much time with me, twice what he gives other patients. He asked me a hundred questions and made me walk back and forth." Foolishly, I persisted: "So what was his opinion about your condition?" Again she answered: "He was very worried about me. He's so sweet to me, he likes me so much. He gives me more time than any other patient. And the nurses all hug me -- they felt so bad for me. They all know me and love me." (This is a direct quote; I jotted it down right after our conversation with an eye to including it in this book.)

As my father-in-law once said with wicked sarcasm and absolute accuracy, "Everybody loves Eda. Just ask her!" Not once do I remember a conversation with Eda in which she didn't tell me how the clerks in the supermarket or the tellers in the bank or the nurses at the hospital or any of the people whom she had encountered that day all loved her and insisted on giving her big hugs. Often when I took her on an errand, I witnessed the hugs she received from tradespeople -- only after Eda reached out and insisted on hugging them first, to my acute embarrassment.

One day I called Eda and asked, "How was your lunch yesterday?" She answered, "There was a very tall and handsome young man sitting at a table across from me. He kept smiling at me and was flirting with me so much through the whole meal that his wife or girlfriend -- she was very beautiful -- got annoyed and said something to him. I felt sorry for her because he was ignoring her and flirting with me. People love me so much everywhere I go, even young people." (Translation: she kept staring at the young man and smiling at him flirtatiously. She probably reminded him of his mother or his grandmother, so he smiled back. His wife/girlfriend probably commented, "I wonder why that old lady keeps staring at us. I wish she'd just stop and eat her lunch, she's making me uncomfortable.")

There is a story that she told to her sister-in-law Eva when the latter came from Australia to visit us in August 2000, which Eva then shared with me. During the war, Eda worked as an accountant for a Russian firm in Poland. The director of the firm fell in love with her. Because she was so good at accounting, they wanted to send her to Russia. She knew that once the Russians got hold of her, they would never let her out. She became very upset and cried a lot. The director, who loved her so much, couldn't stand to see her unhappy, so he intervened on her behalf, and they didn't make her go.

Every summer my mother used to take a vacation at the Lodge of the Four Seasons in Lake of the Ozarks. I would take her to the airport, put her on a plane (this was before 9/11 so one could accompany a passenger directly to the gate) and, at the end of her vacation, I would pick her up and drive her home. For our twenty-fifth anniversary, Bob and I decided to splurge and take a trip sponsored by the Missouri Botanical Garden to the "Gardens of Yorkshire." We were very excited about the prospect and, when our daughters came to spend Thanksgiving with us, we told them about it. Since I was preparing the meal and setting a festive table, the girls went to pick up their grandmother at her apartment. They told her about our plans in the car on the way to our house, and she immediately protested that she needed me to take her to the airport in May, at the exact time that our trip was scheduled. Our daughters pleaded with her not to say anything to us that would spoil our excitement. After all, it was going to be a momentous occasion for us. No sooner had Eda crossed the threshold than she approached me at the sink and said, "You can't go on that trip. I need you to take me to the airport and pick me up when I come back from my vacation."

"Why can't you go a week earlier?" I asked.

"Because it will still be too cold."

"OK, then why can't you go a week later?"

"Because by then it will be too hot and the mosquitoes will be out."

Even knowing Eda as I did, I was taken aback by this utter self-absorption and lack of consideration for her daughter.

I don't mean to give the impression that Eda was cold and unfeeling. At times, when I was upset about something (especially about a boy), she treated me with affection. She would stroke my cheek or my hair tenderly and tell me that it would all work out OK. Generally, this didn't make me feel better. What I really needed was to feel her arms around me with the unstinting commitment of a full-body hug. What I got was a feather-light touch on the cheek. This was a form of affection, but it allowed her to keep a distance between us. The lack of connection left me feeling guilty for feeling unsatisfied. For the most part, however, Eda was too busy or too tired or too preoccupied with her own concerns to pay attention to my "silly little worries."

Self-absorption, egocentrism, was another of Eda's hallmarks. Every scrap of information that my mother imparted became a drama, with her taking center stage, either as star or as victim. Monday nights at the Villas were special for her. Every Monday evening the activities director led a discussion on current events. Eda read the newspaper diligently, listened carefully to several newscasts every day, and made copious notes. She took delight in bragging to me every Tuesday morning that she knew all the answers and was much smarter than the other residents. Then one Tuesday morning she sounded dejected and said she was not going back to the current events sessions any more. When I asked her why, she said that the uppity young leader (who until then had been beautiful and wonderful) had told her she needed to give others a chance to answer some of the questions. Similarly, bridge, arts and crafts, and several other activity groups were embraced and then abandoned when someone expressed displeasure at her attempt to dominate the action.

For every form letter she received, Eda was convinced that someone composed and sent it specifically to her. When I tried to explain that these were just form letters generated by a computer and sent out by the hundreds, she wanted to learn how a computer works. So I took her home with me and gave her a simplified demonstration of how form letters and envelopes are created. I thought she was paying close attention to the screen, but much to my surprise, at the conclusion of my little tutorial, her comment was, "Did you know that you have a wrinkle in the back of your neck? I've never seen anyone with wrinkles there before." (This was all the more interesting because until that day, the only compliment she gave me occasionally was that I had a lovely long neck, like a swan. Suddenly the swan had turned into an ugly duckling!)

Another time I was taking my mother to a department store to buy a coat. When we reached the right floor, I started steering her toward the coat section. But Eda headed toward the nearest cash register, where several customers were waiting in line. She marched right up to the salesperson and inquired, "Could you please tell me where the coats are?" The saleslady replied politely, "I'm busy with a customer right now but if you wait a few minutes, I'll be glad to show you." Undeterred, my mother insisted, "But I want to buy a coat. Could you just show me where they are?" Realizing that it would be simpler just to let my mother have her way, the woman at the front of the line said, "Go ahead, I'll wait." The saleslady led us over to the coat department. At that instant, my mother grabbed her in a big hug and gave her a kiss on the cheek, saying, "You are so kind. I don't know what we would have done without your help." (Need I elaborate on how this made me feel?) Obviously uncomfortable, the saleslady had no choice but to return my mother's hug half-heartedly and to say, "You're very welcome." She then beat a hasty retreat. My mother turned to me and piped, "Did you see how that saleslady hugged me? People are so nice to me. All the salespeople just love me."

On this occasion, I learned a valuable lesson. Terribly embarrassed by Eda's behavior, I started to apologize to the woman who had allowed Eda to cut in front of her. "Don't apologize," said the woman, "we all have mothers." Such a simple statement, but it proved to be so liberating for me! At that moment, I became aware of something that I had never formulated so concretely: people did not hold me responsible for my mother's behavior. Thanks to this epiphany, it was much easier for me to relax when I was around her and to let her be herself. In fact, I learned to apply this new-found revelation to other people in my life, both friends and relatives. Once I realized that I was not responsible for their behavior, I stopped worrying about someone talking too loudly in public or using improper grammar or having poor table manners; I was able to focus instead on the wisdom of their words or the kindness of their actions, which enabled me to enjoy their company.

Time and again Eda told me how jealous all the other residents were of her. Since many of them needed canes or walkers or were confined to wheelchairs, it is not surprising that they often remarked that they wished they could walk like she did. Until the day she had her stroke, her back was always ramrod straight. No mincing, gliding steps for Eda; her determination was always evident in her walk. Instead of being grateful for her good health and understanding the longing expressed by these disabled seniors, Eda constantly complained that she couldn't put up with their jealousy. One night she experienced leg cramps. She called me the next morning to tell me that on the previous evening, a couple of the residents had been eyeing her shapely calves (her words), and she was convinced that her cramps were the result of their giving her the evil eye because they were so jealous.

Eda once told me that when she was fifteen or sixteen, a friend of her father's, who was a family physician, fell in love with her and kissed her and made a pass at her. When she told her sister Dunka (nickname for Dina) about this, Dunka was so jealous that she walked over to Eda and slapped her in the face. I believe that Dunka slapped her, and some jealousy may have played a part in this outburst. But I'm inclined to think that the real reason Dinka slapped her is that Eda persisted in rubbing Dunka's nose in the fact that the doctor (who sounds like a pedophile to me) had chosen *her*. For good measure, Eda probably pointed out all of Dunka's shortcomings and flaunted her own superiority in attracting such a distinguished man. Many a time I've seen Eda operate in this mode, and many a person has been sorely tempted to slap her when she did.

Eda was never overly concerned with fairness, objectivity, accuracy, or rationality. She would bend and twist the truth until it assumed the shape that fit into the point she was trying to make. To her, truth was in the eye of the beholder. We all tend to view "the facts" through a filter of rationalization, but she carried this tendency to an extreme. In the world according to Eda, there were only two kinds of people: the highly astute ones who thought she was elegant, brilliant, beautiful, talented... and the rest of the morons who lacked any vestige of brains, breeding, or discernment. When she told you a story, any event that didn't involve her in a favorable light got left on the cutting room floor. Usually the stories had to do with appearances because for Eda, appearance was everything. Though she was not religious in the conventional sense, Eda did have a religion: she worshipped devoutly at the shrine of the god of appearances. One of the characters in Isabel Allende's novel *Daughter of Fortune* says, "What do you want me to do? My life is built on appearances, not truths." She could easily have been talking about my mother.

In addition to hating wrinkles, Eda looked down on anyone who didn't dress in an "elegant" fashion. I didn't dare wear jeans or anything else comfortable when I went to visit her. *What would the residents say?* Several times she impressed upon me the fact that I needed to dress in a more "elegant" fashion whenever I came to the Villas. Lest I fail to get the message, she always pointed out to me the women and men whose dress was up to her high standards. My mother wouldn't dream of going down to get the mail without dressing to the hilt -- jewelry and all, putting on complete makeup, and fixing her hair. Polyester was Eda's friend in her quest for elegance. You may remember when polyester leisure suits were considered the height of coolness. Eda didn't go so far as to wear a leisure suit, but her closet was filled with polyester pants and blouses, many of which are still in her closet at the nursing home, and I hope that, despite her tragically compromised condition, she still has moments when she feels "elegant" in her polyester duds (she was horrified when I tried to dress her in a sweat suit because the aides had told me that this would make it easier for them to dress and undress her.).

During our first couple of years in New York, my mother made me wear brown, high-top leather shoes. When I complained that the other kids made fun of me because of these shoes, she replied, "Never mind, dear. You'll have slim ankles when you grow up." (It didn't work!) I was puzzled by this fixation on sacrificing comfort for "elegance" until my friend Sandi explained to me that this was common among women of that generation and provenance. Sandi told me that her mother's feet would be blistered and almost bloody when she took off her shoes at the end of the day, but her mother would never consider wearing a larger size because she wanted to be seen as having dainty little feet. I suppose this is the derivation of foot binding in some Asian cultures. With my bunions, I thank my lucky stars that I live in America, where I can wear comfortable flat shoes without committing an unforgivable fashion sin.

Since Eda considered herself a fashion guru, each time a new resident moved into the Villas, Eda would take this poor, unsuspecting victim under her wing and try to teach her how to dress or fix her hair or arrange her apartment. Though she desperately wanted to befriend each new arrival, they invariably started "hanging out" with other groups after some time. Eda never understood that it was her constant criticisms and attempts to change them that drove them away. She always attributed their "desertion" to jealousy on the part of the other residents, who "plotted to steal away all her friends." Her attempts to make herself look smart at their expense only served to drive them away. She never understood this, just as I failed to understand that when I was in school, bragging about my grades didn't endear me to my fellow students.

One summer, when the girls were about six and ten, we spent a couple of weeks with my parents, who were then living in an apartment in Kingston, NY. Eda had invited a neighbor over for tea. Before the woman arrived, Eda coached the girls on what to expect and how to behave. As Eda was preparing the refreshments in the kitchen, Lisa informed the neighbor in a serious tone, "Grandma said that you have an ugly face but that we should be nice to you anyway." Had Eda not put so much emphasis on appearance, it never would have occurred to the girls that the woman did not live up to Eda's idea of attractiveness.

In my mother's eyes, if you were tall, thin, preferably male, dressed formally at all times, and spoke softly and infrequently, and especially if you never disagreed with her, it followed naturally that you were intelligent and kind, possessed of good breeding and impeccable taste. I am female, just under five feet, well rounded, inclined to argue when I feel strongly about a subject, and my preferred outfit consists of jeans, a T-shirt, and tennis shoes. In my mother's eyes, therefore, I was ignorant, unsightly, inconsiderate, rude, and lacking any vestige of taste. When I saw myself through my mother's eyes, I saw a totally worthless human being. This is why my stomach knotted whenever I went to see her and why my visits became less frequent as time went by.

I knew that she wanted me to succeed because she loved me (on her own terms) and she did want me to be happy, but mainly she wanted my success to give her bragging rights. During the eleven years that Bob and I lived in Galveston, I worked as an associate in the office of Research in Medical Education. Through a series of circumstances, I became the co-author of a book on pediatric ECGs published by Little, Brown and Company, and for several years I received royalties on this book. Nothing made Eda happier than when I told her a royalty check had arrived, even if it was only for a couple of dollars. She could then brag to anyone who would listen about her daughter, "the author."

Even then, she did not tell me that she was proud of me for my accomplishments. She never failed to prick my bubble by pointing out how I had failed. In seventh grade, I won the all-school spelling bee. Rushing home, I couldn't wait to show Eda my trophy and hear her praise. What was her response? "You should button your coat and wear your gloves. It's cold outside." My winning essay in the *I Speak for Democracy* contest brought tears to the eyes of our pharmacist but no praise from Eda. If I brought home a college transcript with five As and one B, she immediately fixated on the B and never stopped giving me grief about it: I didn't study enough, all I was interested in was fun and parties and boys. If I brought home all As, it only meant that I was doing the minimum required; I should be reading great literature classics and doing more to develop my mind. Surprisingly, I did get a satisfactory reward after one grueling semester when I loaded up on course work and managed to excel in all my courses. After Eda went into her litany, Dad called me aside and told me, "You study much more than I did, and I made it through medical school. So don't worry about what your mother just said." Since my Dad never contradicted my mother -- he stayed in the background and let her do the childrearing and disciplining -- this was an extraordinary turn of events, and the glow from his praise stayed with me for a long, long time.

Eda thought that she was encouraging me not to rest on my laurels but to push myself to my highest potential. However, the actual result was to make me feel that I could never please her, so why even try? It was only the strong sense of obligation I felt to repay her for all her sacrifices that motivated me to keep on striving to do my best, since my feelings of inferiority convinced me that I would never be successful at anything, no matter how hard or how long I tried. Even though I agree with the school of thought that does not believe you should praise a child just for having a pulse because false praise can have a detrimental effect, I do believe that children of all ages have a need to be affirmed whenever they succeed in doing something that merits their parents' approval.

Eda's attitude toward me was often far more destructive than the mere withholding of approval. She never missed a chance to declare pointedly that I was so obstinate, unyielding, argumentative, etc., etc. that no one could ever love me. I understand now that she was "blaming the victim" – that is, she was rationalizing her inability to feel unconditional love for me by turning me into a person unworthy of such love. I wish I had understood this when I was a child; I would have spared myself many nights of crying myself to sleep. Children assimilate their parents' morals, thoughts, opinions, pronouncements. From these, they derive their feelings of goodness or badness about themselves. Individuals who lack a sense of self-worth, of identity think that they are not acceptable to others. How could I possibly have a positive sense of identity? Where would it have come from?

Maybe Eda was right. Maybe there is something missing from my emotional makeup because I can't comprehend what I call "automatic" or "obligatory" love. Time after time I've seen stories in which long-lost siblings or parents/offsprings who had not seen each other since birth (if ever) are reunited and immediately express heartfelt love for each other. What does this mean? Does it mean that simply because they share some genetic components, they have an instant mutual affection? As I see it, love -- like respect and trust -- is an emotion that evolves from interactions with another person. I need to share some values/ideas/opinions/traits that cause me to connect on an emotional plane before I can feel love toward that person. How can I invest my deepest emotions and make myself vulnerable toward someone whom I've never met, with whom I have never interacted? I can appreciate the unconditional love that a parent feels for a child or a wife feels for her spouse. We love them even if they commit inexcusable acts. We may disapprove strongly of their behavior, but our love is not eroded by that disapproval. But the bond of love precedes the disapproval/disappointment we feel when their comportment breaches our value system. How can I love someone I don't know? Why would I want to trace my lineage and create a family tree if there is no chance that I will ever meet these relatives? They are just names on paper. Does that make me cold, unfeeling, lacking in compassion?

And yet, Eda was proud of me, even if she never told me so. When I cleaned out her apartment after it became evident that she would not return from the nursing home, I found an album with every picture or mention of my name in every publication carefully clipped out and pasted in. It was not unusual for me to hear, when I met one of her friends, that my mother was very proud of me and always bragged about me. This tendency was common in her generation. I have seen many emotional scars grow out of the well-meaning but misguided notion that a parent can brag to relatives, friends, neighbors, even strangers -- but must never, never praise the child directly. Whenever my daughters visited Eda, they would tell me that their grandmother had regaled them with stories about how smart I was and all the wonderful things I had done.

Because she didn't feel responsible for their upbringing, Eda's attitude toward her granddaughters was much less contentious than it was toward me. With them, she was able to behave the way I always wished she could be with me -- she was able to relax, let her guard down, act silly, laugh, and have fun. In front of me I have a letter from Lisa that she wrote in 1991, as I was going through a rough period in my life, that contains an amazingly sensitive, highly insightful depiction of the situation:

"...I love Grandma Eda dearly and she and I have a very special relationship -- it is an ideal grandmother-granddaughter relationship. However, that does not mean I am blind to the way she treats you. The ability our parents have to affect us doesn't change much as we 'grow up.'...Grandma Eda still pulls a lot of your strings. The reasons for why she is so guilt-trip laden, manipulative, and perhaps self-centered are very complicated and I can try to appreciate them, but the effect on you is still the same. Somewhere in you she has planted the seed that you will always fall short -- you aren't kind enough, you don't do enough, you are lucky you found a man to marry you, etc. You may think you have come to terms with this, but it still affects you. You love your parents and you grew up believing that love and respect for your parents is very important (it is). You have also been through a lot as a family and that ties you together in a certain way. She dealt with your father's Alzheimer's and his death much differently than you did, and your feelings towards her are affected by that also. Sometimes when we are talking and you are sharing your feelings with me, I see a rejected and insecure little girl -- it breaks my heart. I wish you could see yourself the way I see you instead of the way she does."

Is it any wonder that I am enormously proud of my daughters (I tell them so at every opportunity) and I consider them to be my closest friends? What a miracle that these superb women grew up "in spite of their parents"!

Notwithstanding her love for her granddaughters, Eda still manifested some of her less admirable traits with them. Ami rarely got to see her grandmother when she was in college, so Eda always claimed that these visits were precious to her and they were what kept her going. To show you how much attention she paid to Ami at those times, I'll relate what Ami once told me. On one of her visits, after the initial greeting, Ami amused herself by not saying one single additional word until it was time to leave. Eda never noticed! In her customary fashion, she asked questions and then immediately jumped in with her own thoughts before Ami had a chance to open her mouth to answer. Maugham might have been talking about Eda when he described one of his characters in *Of Human Bondage:* "...liked to hear himself talk. He was not sensitive to the interest of his listeners, which is the first requisite of the good talker, and he never realized that he was telling people what they knew already." My husband used to say that he could always tell when I was on the phone with my mother because I would just sit with the receiver to my ear without saying a word for prolonged periods of time.

When Ami tearfully revealed to my mother that she was in the process of divorcing her husband, my mother showed where her concern lay with two questions: "Whose name are you going to take? Don't go back to 'Feinstein' because there is so much anti-Semitism these days," and "Who is going to turn my mattress now?" (Ami and her husband had always rotated Eda's mattress when they came to visit.) Needless to say, compassion was not Eda's strong suit.

She used people and saw them only in terms of what they could do for her. After one of her neighbors in the retirement home sustained a multiple fracture of her leg, Eda's comment was, "How could she do that to me? She was the only one I could trust to pick up my mail while I went on my vacation!"

For a number of months she had a "boyfriend" who, even after he moved out of the retirement home, called her twice daily, took her for rides, and always showed great concern for her wellbeing. It was wonderful for me to see her so happy. And, since he listened to all her stories and complaints, I was freed from many hours of having to do the listening, so I liked him sight unseen. Then he became ill and gradually started to lose his physical and mental vigor. For all those months, he had shared her every worry and had reassured her and made her feel good. But as soon as he needed some support from her, she quickly decided that she didn't need to be bothered with his problems, and she dropped him like the proverbial hot potato and refused to have anything more to do with him.

She was manipulative but not mean: she truly believed that what she was doing was for the good of the other person. Throughout my high school years, it was my job to clean our entire house every Saturday after I listened to my morning radio programs. When I say "clean," I mean white-glove quality clean. Mother's justification for making me take on this odious task was that she was trying to teach me to be a good housewife. I would see my classmates pass by outside and know that they were headed for pleasurable activities, and resentment would bubble up inside me. But once Eda decided on a course of action, it was easier to do her bidding than to try to dissuade her, especially since I didn't know how to challenge her without making her angry.

When she decided that I ought to start cooking dinners so that I would learn how to cook, I made a beef stew that my father said was the best he had ever tasted. Armed with his commendation, I was able to talk her out of making me take on this responsibility as well. I would have been much less resentful if she had been honest with me and had explained to me that we couldn't afford to hire help and the work was too much for her. Appeals to my better nature have invariably inspired me to pitch in and give it my all. When I worked in a clothing store where I had to punch a time clock, I never put in any extra time. Even if I was in the middle of negotiating a lucrative sale when my time was up, I simply transferred the client to another sales person and went home. When my boss's attitude at the Medical School was, "I trust you to get the job done competently in whatever amount of time you need," I willingly spent countless extra hours after my regular work day, simply because I was so motivated to show him that his faith in me was not misplaced. Eda never understood this concept. Once again, false pride and appearances - -and the fear that I would tell someone and then people would find out we were not well-to-do -- kept her from taking the forthright approach. In her mind, Dr. Benton -- and by extension, Mrs. Dr. Benton -- could gain the respect of the townspeople only by projecting an image of affluence and elegance, regardless of reality.

Her eyesight was another weapon Eda used to get me to do things for her. She would demand that I select greeting cards, grocery items, and anything else she might need in the store (and would then unfailingly proceed to tell me how awful my choices were) because she couldn't see well. Yet if there was a white thread out of place on the white collar of my blouse, her eagle eye would spot it immediately, even from some distance away. Our cousin Dorothy, who has never uttered an unkind word about anyone, told me the story of one time when she was in St. Louis to visit her son's family while Bob and I were out of town. They all took Eda out to dinner at a restaurant where the lighting was rather dim. Everyone at the table whipped out their glasses to read the menu -- everyone, that is, except Eda, who had no difficulty at all reading it without glasses!

Eventually, Eda did lose the vision in her right eye. Of course, it happened during one of the rare times when Bob and I were taking a trip. When we arrived home, there was a frantic message on our answering machine. I immediately called my mother, who told me that she had a strange sensation in her eye during the afternoon and that she now couldn't see out of that eye. Alarmed, Bob called a retina specialist, who happened to be a friend of ours. He kindly offered to go back to the office and check mother out right away. I called her back to tell her that I was coming to pick her up and drive her to the doctor but, to my surprise, she said that she was already in her nightgown and didn't want to get dressed and make herself presentable at that time. I tried to impress upon her that time was of the essence and that there might be something the doctor could give her to reverse the blindness if he saw her right away, but she was dogged in her insistence that she wanted to wait until morning (her excuse was that she didn't want to bother the doctor, but I knew that she didn't want him to see her looking less than her best.). Because I had been away from the office for several days, it was important for me to go to work that morning to deal with the mail and messages that had accumulated during my absence. Besides, the doctor had surgical cases in the morning. I knew that having waited so many hours, it didn't matter whether I took her to see him first thing in the morning or later in the day, so I waited until I got home in the early afternoon to take her. Never did I suspect that she would blame me forever for her loss of vision because I didn't take her in the morning. Months later, when I told Eda that I had taken my kitty to the vet early in the morning because it was an emergency, Eda said plaintively, "Too bad I'm not a cat. Maybe then you would have taken me to the doctor in time to save my eyesight."

Guilt was a sword Eda wielded with consummate skill. Legend has it that every Jewish mother is a travel agent for guilt trips (this tenet has long been a staple of the comedy circuit), but my mother surpassed them all. I could fill this volume with examples, but I will limit myself to one revealing illustration. One day, I was driving my mother home after having just chased around to a zillion stores to find all the specific items she said she needed. She had been particularly finicky that day, and I was rushing because I had some errands I needed to run for my family. Eda started harping on how all the other daughters take such good care of their mothers who lived in her residence and how she was all alone, with no one to take care of her. Talk about guilt trips! I knew she just wanted to make me feel guilty so that I would come to see her more often and spend more time letting her show me for the umpteenth time how she conducts her weird system of bookkeeping (more on that later), but my first thought was, "If you're so all alone and have no one to help you, why am I wasting my time coming to see you almost every day and doing all this for you instead of spending more time with my family or doing something I enjoy?" Of course, I kept trying to meet her needs because, after all, I did love her and, above all, I owed her.

With Eda as my model, I became a master at using guilt on everyone -- my friends, my husband, my children. It enabled me to win many battles, but oddly enough, none of those victories gave me any satisfaction. It took a year of intensive counseling at age fifty to make me realize that I had been blindly following my mother's example, even though this was not a natural way for me to behave and it made me very uncomfortable. If there were one thing I could do over in the way I raised my daughters, I would eliminate guilt from my toolbox of parental devices. Guilt is not a teaching tool. It is cruel, it undermines self-esteem, it erodes morale, and it gives rise to bitter resentments. That also applies to the concept of "survivor guilt." Living with the burden of survivor guilt often leads to feelings of depression, thoughts of suicide, and PTSD-like symptoms. I believe instead in "survivor gratitude." I thank whatever powers decreed that I should live when millions around me were dying. I believe that the best way to show my gratitude is to make the most of my life, to spread as much positive energy in the world as I possibly can.

Laying blame has never resolved a conflict; it only serves to set up an adversarial relationship, which then acts as a roadblock to any constructive problem solving. I can best make my point by setting up a little scenario: I've made a date with my friend to meet at XYZ restaurant at 7:00 pm on Tuesday. I arrive on time; she doesn't show up. When I speak to her later, she says, "Oh, I'm sorry. I thought we said Wednesday night." If I'm in Eda-mode, my response is: "How could you possibly get it wrong? We talked about it, and I wrote it down on my calendar. I waited for you for over an hour. I was so hungry that I almost fainted. The waitresses all felt so sorry for me and offered to get me something, but I thought you'd show up at any moment, so I refused. If I had known you weren't coming, I wouldn't have wasted my time going there and waiting for you when I have a million things I could have done instead." A year of counseling and several decades of life have taught me that a more productive way of handling the situation and maintaining my friendship would be to say something like: "Maybe I misunderstood or wrote down the wrong day on my calendar. I have an idea. Next time we make a date, let's send each other an email. That way we'll have some written backup."

As to Eda's bookkeeping, that's another sore subject for me. She didn't trust any financial institution, so she had small accounts in several banks and a little money in a number of bond funds. She also didn't trust the U.S. mail, so she did all her banking in person. The van drivers at the Villas thought she was very wealthy because she went to banks with such frequency, and she did nothing to dispel this grand illusion. She managed her finances herself, spending countless hours every day in painstakingly writing down everything in notebooks and on assorted slips of paper, indexing and cross-indexing every holding and every transaction in multiple formats, adding the figures over and over again on her calculator. She thought this entitled her to announce to one and all that she was a businesswoman. Though at first I believed her plaintive protests that it was all too much for her and I offered to take over this burden, I soon came to realize that this "accounting job" gave her life a purpose and that she really needed this distraction from thinking about her situation and her future.

Since she also didn't trust the maids or the service people who had access to her apartment, she would conceal all these notebooks and slips of paper, along with small sums of cash, in various hiding places in her dressers and closets. I still have the little yellow post-it that she attached to each "treasure": "Don't touch, as I'll know." Every time I came to visit her, she would subject me to a catechism on where she had squirreled away each of these notebooks and envelopes and what they all contained. She shuffled them around continually, so there was a new series of hiding places to show me during almost every visit (after a while, she started writing herself little notes in Polish shorthand so that she could keep track of all the hiding places). As if this weren't unpleasant enough, she would then insist on quizzing me about every detail. I can't begin to describe how painful and degrading this process was for me and how I dreaded going to see her when I knew this trial by fire awaited me! Invariably I would forget something, and she would pounce on me with victorious self-righteousness. It seemed to me that she put me through this exercise just to humiliate me, but eventually I realized that she was consumed by her preoccupation with money.

It is not surprising that money was of such great importance for her. We came to this country with nothing, and we lived on charity during our first couple of years here. Even after my Dad established his medical practice, we would never become wealthy, given that he charged so little for office visits and house calls. Many of his patients could not afford to pay him in cash, so he regularly accepted compensation in the form of chickens, eggs, flowers -- anything that the farmers in the outlying areas could give him, and sometimes no payment at all. Furthermore, like many in his profession, he was a terrible businessman. I have to give his wife a lot of credit for managing the household in such a way that they could afford to pay the mortgage, send me to college, do a little traveling, and buy a new car every couple of years. After my father passed away, Eda made some wise investments so that there is still enough money left to pay for her nursing home and for the supplies she needs.

Actually, if Eda realized that her hard-earned savings are all being used to pay for nursing home care, she would probably find a way to end her life. She deprived herself all those years, scrimping and saving in every possible way, so that she could leave some money for her granddaughters after she passed away. Somehow she felt that if she gave them money, they would remember her with more love. From time to time, she gave the girls some money when they were in graduate school. She always made sure that I was aware of her magnanimity. You've heard of anonymous benefactors? Eda was the exact counterpart. One year, when Lisa was coming home for their annual joint birthday celebration, Eda called during a time when she knew I would be at work so that she could leave the following message on the answering machine: "When you see Lisa, please give her the message that I am going to give her $200 for her birthday so you and she can go shopping for some nice things for her." While giving Lisa the money for her birthday was a nice thing for my mother to do, she knew that I would be calling her that afternoon, and she could have told me then. Better yet, she could have told Lisa directly, since Lisa always called her soon after she arrived in town. But Eda didn't want to miss an opportunity to make sure I knew of her generosity, and I'm certain that she hoped that Bob would retrieve the message so that he would know as well. This was vintage Eda!

Concerns about money caused Eda the most sleepless nights, and her pet peeve was the way her sister-in-law Eva spent the money that Eda sent her. From the stories that circulated, Eva's son and daughter-in-law were always in dire straits: either they were on the verge of being evicted for not paying their mortgage or they couldn't afford necessary medications for one of their eight children, or some such crisis was always imminent. Eva would feel sorry for them and give them the money that Eda kept sending her. Then Eda would fret incessantly about the fact that Eva gave the money to her son and daughter-in-law who, according to Eda, wasted it on frivolous things like toys for the kids, electronic gadgets, or large dinner parties instead of using it for sensible expenses. I tried to tell Eda, "You have two choices: either don't send Eva any more checks or, if you keep sending her money, resign yourself to the fact that it's hers to do with as she pleases and don't even ask her how she spent it." Invariably Eda's response was, "I can't stop sending her money because she'll wind up in the poor house. But how can she be so foolish as to give it to those kids? Your father and I denied ourselves so much all our lives and we saved the money carefully, and now look at how she throws it away!" As I've said before, once Eda fixated on something, there was no changing her mind.

Every so often she would call me to tell me that the staff was taking the residents to such a nice lunch or to the theater, but she didn't sign up because it cost $10 or $20. I would say, "If you left the girls $20 more or less, do you think it would really affect their lifestyles?" And she would say "No." And I would say, "But it would make a big difference in your life if you went out and had a good time." And she would say, "When you explain it like that, it makes a lot of sense." And I would think, "Eureka! I finally got through to her!" But the following week she would call me and say, "They went to lunch in a beautiful restaurant that had lots of flowers, and they all raved about it when they got back. But I didn't go because it cost $12." And I would think to myself, "Why do I even try?!"

During her years at the senior residence, every telephone conversation with Eda had several predictable elements:

1) her wrinkles (getting worse by the day);
2) my wrinkles (getting worse by the minute);
3) she didn't sleep all night -- again;
4) she was so frightened/worried about ___ (fill in the blank -- there was always something) that it's a wonder she didn't get a stroke or a heart attack;
5) she was terribly upset because the doctor/lawyer/accountant/restaurant/store had charged her so much;
6) everybody (doctor/lawyer/accountant/bank teller/residence staff/store clerk) loved her so much and always gave her hugs and kisses;
7) everyone was jealous of her (especially her friends, whom she loved to hate).

My mother was a one-dimensional person. By that I mean she rarely, if ever, acknowledged that there is more than one side to every issue. In her simplistic view, all the problems of the world could be solved very easily. Too much violence? Just take guns away from everybody; problem solved. You want an abortion? No one has the right to tell you that you can't have one, and anyone who says otherwise is just plain stupid. In my mother's world view, there are two kinds of people: the brilliant, cultured, compassionate ones who always agree with her and flatter her; and the ignorant, rude, worthless ones who have the gall to voice an opinion that does not meet with her approval. And it would make your head spin to see how quickly they can change sides. A wonderful friend from Peru was our house guest for a few days. Since Eda was returning from one of her Lake of the Ozarks vacations during Consuelo's visit, I took her with me to the airport to pick up Eda. The two immediately hit it off and chatted as if they had been long-time friends while we waited for the luggage. As Eda's little yellow suitcase made its way toward us on the conveyor belt, I reached out to pick it up and carry it out to the parked car. Eda had a fit, insisting that the suitcase was much too heavy for me to carry, I would get a hernia, I should find a porter to carry it out for us. I assured Eda that I work out with weights heavier than her little suitcase, but she fretted and fumed all the way home about what a stubborn and disobedient child I am. The next time I talked to Eda, she was full of praise for our elegant and refined friend. However, when I told her that Consuelo had agreed with me about the suitcase and thought Eda had made an unnecessary fuss about the issue (I thought this would convince Eda that maybe I could be right about something once in a while!), she surprised me by saying, "What do I care what some foreigner thinks of me? Her English is terrible and her accent is even worse than mine."

Eda's sister-in-law Eva is one of the most optimistic, positive, loving, and caring people on this planet; you would never know that she had survived Auschwitz if you didn't see the numbers tattooed on her forearm. From the time Milek, Eda's brother, brought her into our family, Eda adored Eva. Then, a few years ago, Eva learned that she could put in a slave labor reparation claim against the Swiss government, and in order to do so, she requested some family information. Instantly Eda became fully convinced that Eva was trying to cause her to have a stroke so that she could get her hands on the money Eda had promised to leave in her will. Not only that, Eda told me that she was sure Eva had driven her own mother to her death through her meanness and had caused Eda's brother to have a heart attack because of her spendthrift habits (years ago Eva had bragged that she had bought an expensive leather jacket for Milek, and this sin was now produced as evidence). The fact that Eva immediately agreed to drop the claim and apologized profusely as soon as she realized this matter was upsetting Eda had no bearing whatsoever on Eda's fury. After a lifetime of common suffering and intense family love for my aunt Eva, Eda suddenly turned all her anger and scorn and vengeful feelings upon Eva because she had done something that my mother considered unwarranted.

To be fair to Eda, her violent emotions in this instance arose out of fear that someone in authority would discover her past and she, along with her family, would be subjected to severe punishment or deportation. Such extreme fear may be incomprehensible unless you have lived under a regime where at any time, for any reason -- or for no reason at all -- your door could be kicked in, you and your loved ones could be dragged out of bed, shoved down the street, and never be seen or heard from again. If you witnessed such scenes being enacted over and over again, even if you were not one of the victims, you lived in constant terror, never knowing when it would be your turn. It is extremely difficult, if not impossible, to surmount fear of this magnitude.

Today I noticed that the license plate on the car in front of me read: "WHT IF." My brain automatically did an immediate word association: "Eda." Here is an example of how the "what if" game is played: for conducting her "financial business," Eda wanted a small desk to put into a corner of her living room. She had measured the space carefully so that she knew precisely what size would fit into that area. And so we set off on another one of our exhausting shopping expeditions to find exactly what she wanted. After several hours of searching through just about every furniture store in the vicinity, she found the perfect desk at the right price. While she paid for it, I drove around to the loading dock, and one of the employees helped me load it into my SUV. Now began the game part. As we drove home, Eda started worrying:

"What if Jack [the handyman] isn't around to help us get it upstairs?"

"Then we'll borrow their hand truck and I'll do it myself."

"What if it doesn't fit through the front door? It's very narrow."

"Then they will open the other half of the front door."

"What if it doesn't fit into the elevator?"

"They move big pieces of furniture in that elevator, so I'm sure this little desk will fit."

"What if it doesn't look right in that corner of the room?"

"Then we'll return it to the store."

"What if you're too busy to go back to the store with me?"

On and on it went -- you get the idea. The "what if" player is always facing a thousand worries, long before one appears on the horizon, says Maeve Binchy in *Light a Penny Candle*.

Another game that Eda played like a champion was the "yes but" routine. It goes something like this:

Eda: A very distinguished young man came to talk to us and he recommended that we buy this stock. Here is the literature he gave us. What do you think, Bob? Is it a good investment? Should I buy it?

Bob (after looking over the prospectus): It looks like a good, solid company, and they certainly have been paying a very good dividend.

Eda: Yes, but it's not tax exempt.

Bob: Then maybe you should look into investing in a municipal bond fund.

Eda: Yes, but they're not insured. What if it goes down? I can't afford to lose money at my age.

Bob: Then maybe you should put your money into treasury bills.

Eda: Yes, but they pay so little. I'd like to get some return for my money.

Bob: Then maybe you should buy a CD.

Eda: Yes, but you have to tie up your money for such a long time to get a decent yield. What if interest rates go up in the meantime? Besides, I need more liquidity.

Bob: You could put your money into a prime money market.

Eda: Yes, but they give you such limited check writing privileges. I need to be able to write more checks for smaller amounts.

Bob: I'm going to lie down. You've given me a headache.

Game over.

Sometimes it seemed that the fates conspired against me so that I could do nothing right for Eda. She liked the Paloma Picasso brand of perfume and told me that she got lots of compliments whenever she wore it. For her birthday one year I gave her a good-sized (and expensive) flask of this perfume. She called me a few days later to tell me she didn't like the smell. "Look, mother, it's exactly the same as the one you had before that you liked so well." "No," she said, "it doesn't smell the same." So I took her to the department store to return it, thinking that she didn't like it just because I was the one who had given it to her. But when she told her story to the salesperson, the woman confirmed that the company had recently changed the formulation of the scent.

Another time, when Eda still lived in Kingston, she mentioned to me that she had broken the tumbler she used in the bathroom and was having a hard time finding a pink one to replace it. I spent the better part of one day looking in all the stores for a pink tumbler, and I was overjoyed when I finally found one that I thought she would like. I spent another couple of hours packing it and waiting in line at the post office to ship it to her. When I got home, one of the girls remarked, "I wonder how long it will be before she returns it." Sure enough, a week later it came back -- the base was too wide to fit into the holder above her sink. No matter how hard I tried, there was just no way I could get it right! I didn't realize at the time that the reason I was so devastated had nothing to do with the pink bathroom cup that didn't fit into the holder or the pretty kitchen towel I had enclosed in the package that was not absorbent enough. For the umpteenth time, I felt that Eda was rejecting *me*.

Everyone wants their friends to like their suggestions, but whenever I recommend a movie or a book or a restaurant, I am disproportionately crushed if they don't like it or elated if they express approval. Why does it matter so much? For me, it's a question of rejection or validation of *me*. People who are insecure, who do not have a positive self-image find it hard to divorce criticism of an action or a behavior from condemnation of the entire person. In other words, it is difficult for them to understand that I may disapprove of what you did at a certain time, but I still think you are a good person and I still like you. As a friend explained it to me once, "It's hard for me to say I'm sorry because that means I messed up, which means that I'm a screw-up and you won't like/love me any more." On the other hand, I'm always apologizing because I am convinced that I have done or said something wrong, that it's my fault things are not going well. This means that I have to make you think I'm a worthwhile person so that you will still be my friend.

As I've mentioned before, my mother loved to entertain so she could show off her skills. Everything she served was a work of art, and her guests often remarked that her creations were too pretty to eat. I loathed those parties, or the preparation that went into them! Whenever she went into a frenzy of baking and cooking and cleaning, she became increasingly tense and demanding. It was always my job, among other things, to make paper-thin slices of the cucumbers, mushrooms, radishes, and other vegetables that she used for garnishes. How I yearned just once to hear the words, "Good job!" But it was not to be. Invariably she would grab the knife out of my hand, reprimanding me sharply either for taking too much time or for not making the slices the way she wanted me to. Try as I might, I could **NEVER** move as quickly as she wished, the slices were never at a **GOOD** angle, or they were never thin **ENOUGH** to suit her. I would walk forever in the shadow of this failure to measure up.

Recently I read an article about how a mother's words affect the daughter's self-image. They certainly do. When I was pregnant with my daughters, I gained a lot of weight, and I had a hard time losing the weight after they were born. One day my mother was walking behind me. She made the comment, "That's a pretty pair of pants. They would be much prettier if they were several sizes smaller." That did it! I started working out at the gym and nearly starving myself. I told the coach at the gym that if he could get me down to 100 pounds, I would parade down Main Street in a bikini even if the temperature was 20 below (we lived in Ann Arbor at the time). My mother's comment irked me so much that not only did I go down to 100, but I actually brought my weight down from 156 pounds to 89 (No, the coach didn't make me do my bikini walk!). It was only when people started telling me that I looked like a refugee -- my face was all eyes -- that I regained my sanity and started maintaining a weight that is reasonable for me. Today we know about anorexia, and the pundits would say that I was using it to take charge of the one variable that I was able to control, since I had no power over my mother's attitude toward me. In the mid-60s, this was not commonly understood.

I understand that we give flowers to sick people in order to bring some cheer into their lives during difficult times, but I have never understood the practice of bringing or sending flowers to people after they have died. (Yes, I know it is for the benefit of the mourners.) To me, it makes more sense to give the flowers to someone who is still alive and can enjoy them. That is why I made it a point to bring some flowers from my garden to Eda every time I went to see her. In the beginning, she used to smell them and tell me how beautiful they were and put them in a vase on her table. After some time, when we were making plans for all her errands or all the things she wanted to "teach" me, she would say, "Don't bother to bring flowers. I don't have time to prepare a vase with water for them." I always ignored this admonition because I knew that after I left, she would enjoy looking at the flowers that brightened her apartment. After all, how much time does it take to fill a vase with water? I felt that she just could not give me the pleasure of knowing that I had done something good for her.

It seems that every encounter with Eda ended in an argument. She would then tell me that she had to take a tranquilizer every time we got together. I would feel terribly guilty and berate myself for not being able to just listen and not react to her words. I was always apologizing, either verbally or in writing. A few days ago, as I was going through some papers, I came across a folder that contained a series of letters we had written to each other at one of those times when feelings ran high and telephone conversations proved unsatisfactory. I would like to share with you excerpts from these letters because they demonstrate so clearly how hard we tried to communicate and how miserably we failed because each of us was focused on justifying her own position.

> April 11, 1990
> Dear Mother,
> I'm sorry that we ended last night with a little argument. I always feel so awful when this happens. It seems that whenever we try to talk about a sensitive

subject, we always get side-tracked with these little "discussions" and we never really address the important things. Since it is so important to me that you understand why I told you the things I said, I thought I would try to express myself in writing.

First of all, I want you to know that what I said was in no way meant as an attack on you. Believe me, the last thing I would ever want to do is to hurt your feelings. The only reason I tried to convey my feelings to you is to eliminate a source of tension between us and to improve our relationship.

I realize that everything you say to me is for a good reason and is completely justified. I appreciate the fact that your main concern is for my welfare. The problem stems from the fact that it is all based on what <u>you</u> want for me or what <u>you</u> would do if you were in my place, without any respect for my rights to make decisions about <u>my</u> life and to live it <u>my own way</u>. ...Being supportive does not mean simply expressing approval of those actions that you would undertake yourself; that's the easy part. It means understanding and accepting the fact that even if you would do things differently with your life, each adult has the right to do things the way he thinks is best for him, as long as he does not harm anyone or take anything away from anyone.

[Note: I changed my mind about sending her this letter, and I did not mail it until I enclosed it in the one below.]

April 14, 1990
Dear Mother,

Enclosed is a copy of the letter that I felt compelled to write to you because when I tried to explain how I felt [on the telephone]... you kept jumping in and justifying your actions -- that you were concerned about me, that I'm your only daughter, that you did it only because you love me, etc. And so we got into another one of our arguments, and I went home feeling so awful and guilty about having upset you that I sat right down and wrote you the letter to explain that I did not mean to hurt you. And here I am again in the same position -- only this time I'm the one who interrupted you, and for that I'm sorry.

... When you first came to St. Louis, I felt responsible for your happiness and I wanted desperately for us to be friends. I guess I pushed you too hard and was not sensitive enough to the fact that your priorities were different than what I wished for you. As a result, we frequently wound up in disputes and afterwards you would be terribly upset and I would feel very guilty.

... We are all human beings and we should not expect perfection from ourselves or from others. Let's just love and accept each other for what we are and for all the good qualities we possess, instead of always trying to find the imperfections, OK?

April 18, 1990
Dearest Ellen,

I said that I won't reply with a letter and I don't intend to. Our last argument left me weak and sick at heart. You wouldn't let me explain and tried to side-track me. I became hysterical. Ellen, I feel deprived of my dignity. ...Since you accused me several times of words that are against my integrity I made a decision long ago not to let it go any further and I said simply & honestly "it is a lie." Now came again your reaction "I am a liar?" I don't know anything about you & your life to make such a statement. I only tried to react in a drastic way to the words you accused me of in order not to lose my self-respect. ...I can't be so bad if so many young people so lovingly cling to me. ...Try to be more forgiving & understanding and you won't be afraid to come to me.

April 22, 1990
Dear Mother,
Thank you very much for your letter. It's always good to be able to express one's feelings and to clear up any misunderstandings. That's why I'm breaking my pledge to leave the past in the past and I'm writing one last time. From your questions and your reaction to my last letter, I realized that I had not expressed myself well and had given you a false impression of my intentions.
... In response to your letter, you are right: I sometimes attribute words to you that are not the actual words that are used. But people perceive messages in addition to the words that are used, and that is the message that comes across to me. If I have misinterpreted your intentions, I apologize. I will make a greater effort in the future to listen more closely to what you say.
... I would do anything to avoid seeing you as upset as you were last week. That's why I'm going to try very hard to put the past behind us (after all, we can't change the past) and to look forward. Let's keep remembering that today is the first day of the rest of our lives.

April 28, 1990
Dear Ellen,
I finally red [sic] your letter. ...I thank you also for listening once to me on the telephone. Perhaps you will learn to understand that when things concern me your judgment can not prevail but mine should be taken into consideration. This would eliminate my frustration which usually follows.

... I know that you are a caring daughter. It is possible that my nature is such that I don't enjoy being overpowered. ...No more letters, I need peace!

It took this conversation in writing to make me understand that I was doing to my mother exactly the same thing that got me so upset when she did it to me. I was aware that she didn't have many good, healthy, carefree years left, and I was fixated on how I could help her to enjoy those "golden years." So I kept pushing her to get out more and to take part in more of the activities that I thought she would enjoy. In doing so, I did not realize that I was imposing my will on her; I was not allowing her to choose how she wanted to spend her time and/or money. Understandably, this made her feel that I did not respect her wishes or her right to make her own decisions about her life. This exchange of letters, along with counseling, made a big difference in our relationship. I stopped trying to fix everything for Eda, and I began to listen to what she had to say. Once I started reacting to her complaints with a comment like "that must be so difficult for you," we were able to spend time together without arguments, accusations, or hard feelings.

From the time my Dad arrived in St. Louis, he was in a vegetative state. Whenever I found a few free moments, I would run to the nursing home to visit him. Unlike Eda, I did not make a production out of my visits. While she made sure that every nurse and aide was aware of her presence, I would slip in quietly, sit by his beside and talk to him for a few minutes, then I would go on my way. On April 16, 1987, I had just finished bowling with my league and was starting to head home. Suddenly a strange feeling came over me, and I turned the car around and headed for the nursing home. Nothing was different. Dad looked just the same -- still and pale -- and yet I felt the need to say good-bye to him. Before dawn the next morning, I woke up to find that my pillow was wet with tears that I had shed in my sleep; I looked at the alarm clock and went back to sleep. Later that morning the nursing home called me to inform me that Dad had passed away at the exact moment when I had woken up in tears. The director of the nursing home thought that I should be the one to break the news to mother. When I arrived at her apartment, she was in the process of vacuuming. I told her as gently as I could, and I held her while she cried; I couldn't afford the luxury of tears because there were so many arrangements that needed to be made. I guided her through all that had to be done that dreadful day, and I stayed with her until she went to bed that evening. When I got home, I sat down at the typewriter and the following poem seemed to flow directly from my heart to the keyboard:

He was a gentle man,
Soft-spoken and sincere,
With wisdom and compassion
He healed both souls and bodies.

A man of dignity,
A dedicated doctor,
Yet with a lively wit
That sparked the conversation.

A fair disciplinarian
He knew when to be stern,
But warmth and generosity
Affected each decision.

He was an upright man,
Adhering to his principles,
And he earned great respect
From all who ever knew him.

He was a loving man,

Devoted to his family,
And we who loved him so
Will cherish every memory
Of this truly great man.

On impulse, I submitted it to the little monthly newsletter published by the Villas because, even though the poem may be sadly lacking in structure and form, I wanted everyone to know what kind of man my father had been before Alzheimer's robbed him of all these stellar qualities. Even a complete stranger, upon reading this poem, would have some idea about how I felt about my Dad. I adored my father. One of my most vivid images of my Dad is his beautiful, melodious whistle. A few years ago, Walmart ran an ad campaign in which the smiley face would puff out his cheeks and make a tuneful whistle. I would get a catch in my throat because it sounded so much like my Dad whistling. I asked him to teach me to whistle, and he did. Of course, Eda was not pleased -- it was not lady-like and I would get wrinkles around my mouth. Music is constantly running through my head. I wish I could sing, but the sounds that come out of my mouth are woefully different from the messages that my brain sends out. So I go through the day whistling under my breath whenever I'm absorbed in thinking or working. Yes, I have lines around my mouth; I think of them as a tribute to my Dad's teaching, and I feel a pang of love and yearning for him.

And yet, in subsequent years, Eda would claim repeatedly that I didn't care about Leon and that I had never gone to visit him. According to her, she was all alone in caring for him when he was alive as well as when he died; I was no help to her at all. Why do I feel such a painful stab whenever I think about her bitter -- and, to my mind, undeserved -- accusations? I wish I could be more like my father. Leon had a marvelous capacity for insulating himself against Eda's little barbs and annoying habits. He would read his medical journals while she chattered at him non-stop. She was always cold, so she would turn the thermostat up. Without saying a word, he would go turn it down. This daily ballet symbolizes the way in which they would accommodate each other, keeping the peace and avoiding hurt feelings.

In going through Eda's belongings when I cleaned out her apartment after it became clear that, sadly, she would not be leaving the nursing home, I found the transcript of an interview with a young woman named Erin; the interview was a project she did for her anthropology course in 1993. This interview is so revelatory of Eda's thought processes and personality that I would like to quote from it at length. It can serve as a kind of summary and give a picture of Eda through her own words, from the perspective of an unbiased observer. From the tone of her summary, I gather that Erin started out to do a project on the cultural insights of someone with a Polish-Jewish heritage, but in typical fashion, Eda turned the interview around to focus the spotlight on herself, so that Erin had to preface her analysis of the interview by saying that "the approach taken will differ from what might be expected." And again, "I attempted to glean as much information as I could about Gita's [the name Erin used for Eda] Jewish and Polish heritage, but to each question she gave one of two pat answers, 'Oh, I can't remember, that was such a long time ago,' or 'I'm American now, that doesn't matter!'"

I gather that Eda's need to talk about herself trumped her reticence to reveal anything about her past, and she allowed this bright young woman to interview her. But as usual, Eda disclosed little factual information. To begin with, she asked Erin to use made-up names for herself and for Leon in order to protect their identities. The first indication of Eda's vanity is her refusal to reveal her age. Erin writes: "[D]uring our interview Gita [the name she used for this purpose] withheld some information on how long she lived in certain areas, so that I would be unable to piece together her precise age." It was terribly important to Eda that no one ever know her real age. She even gave me the text of what she wanted in her obituary, stressing that her age at the time of death was not to appear anywhere. Erin picked up on this: "She made several references to her youthfulness during our interview. For instance, Gita would not tell me her age because she said it didn't matter -- the age she feels is what matters and she feels *young*. Gita told me that when no one else is in the hallway outside her apartment, she would run up and down it just like a child, to prove that she is still young. Also, except for letters and phone calls, Gita does not socialize with any of her life-long, elderly friends. She prefers instead to go out with her 'young' friends, of whom she has many."

Early in the interview, Eda spoke about her mastery of many languages and her "knack" for numbers. To speak with Eda was to hear how "cultured" she was, how she could recite poetry by heart, how she was doing translations of German and Russian masterpieces. Erin says, "She particularly took pride in telling me of the years she spent in Germany. She showed me numerous pictures and postcards, memorabilia, and so on. She also read pieces of German poetry to me." Eda also told Erin that had they not had a child, she would have "gone to the United Nations to seek employment, hopefully putting her language skills to use. Gita instead stayed home to care for their child. But, Gita's language skills were not wasted during those years. She spent her spare time pouring [sic] over the New York Times -- looking up every word in the dictionary in order to learn yet another language -- English."

Whether the question was never raised or whether Eda deflected it the way she did so many others, there is no explanation how this child suddenly came into Eda and Leon's lives. There is just the one sentence: "By this time [1949] Gita and Abe were the parents of a young daughter." She went on to say that the daughter eventually married and had two daughters of her own. As an example of how much she and Leon traveled during their lives together, she told

Erin that no matter where her two granddaughters are in the country, she flies to see them on their birthdays. This is only partially true. Since Eda's birthday is on July 4th and Lisa's is on July 3rd, we had a joint celebration for them for many years. During the years that Bob was in graduate school and our finances were very tight, Eda and Leon would fly to Ann Arbor to be with us for the celebration. But from the time Lisa was about six years old, we were the ones who flew to their new home in Kingston, where Leon was working at the hospital on a part-time basis.

Eda told of her extensive travels and showed off her valuable "fine items" in order to impress Erin with her "high socioeconomic status that she has enjoyed most of her life." Wealth, culture, elegance, youthfulness -- these are the values that Eda treasured above all else, and no matter what, this is the image she tried to project. It has always been central to her agenda that no one must ever appear superior to her in these aspects. Anything that didn't fit into this facade was filtered out of the conversation.

Eda clothed herself with the mantle of Leon's status as a physician. Take this sentence from Erin's report: "Due to Abe's [the name she used for Leon] status as a physician, the couple was taken in and protected (by whom Gita would not say) when Hitler's slaughter of the Jewish race began." While she disclosed to Erin that her immediate family, except for one brother, was killed, "Gita was reluctant to talk much about this period of her life... saying only 'No one should know of such horrors.'" These answers are similar to the ones I got whenever I tried to question Eda about the past. Small wonder that it took me so long -- almost *too* long -- to get any information out of her so that I would know something about where I came from. I hesitated to ask about my family for a few reasons. For one thing, I thought it would be too painful for Eda to talk about all that she had lost. Another reason was that I didn't understand the concept of "family." I had never shared laughter or tears or hugs or secrets with aunts or uncles (except for Milek and Eva) or cousins or grandparents. I didn't really care who begat whom. Genealogy, or Jewish geography as we sometimes call it, holds no interest for me. Perhaps it is true that a part of me is cold and unfeeling. When you've had to stifle and turn off your feelings as often as I had to do during my formative years, you are bound to lose some of your ability to connect with people, especially with those who are strangers to you. I care deeply, lovingly, unsparingly for my friends and for those family members with whom I've had a chance to interact. I can only muster curiosity but no particular affection for those with whom I've never had any contact, even if we share a bit of common DNA. That is why I was able to sit in a courtroom and repudiate my own father.

I had never met Joseph, or Juzek, as he was called. Apparently he had shown no interest in connecting with me once he gave me up to Eda and Leon. In 1952, an agreement was signed between West Germany and Israel to indemnify Jewish people for the damages caused by Germany through the Holocaust. West Germany paid Israel a sum of three billion marks over the next fourteen years. Joseph was living in Israel and when he found out that he was entitled to substantial reparations for members of his immediate family who were Holocaust survivors, he wanted to reclaim me as his daughter. Since I was away at college in Ann Arbor, I was not privy to the negotiations that took place between him and my parents. One day I was summoned home and, with great trepidation, Eda told me that I was adopted and that my birth father wanted to reclaim me for the purpose of collecting a large sum of money. If I acknowledged him as my father, I would be taken away from Eda and Leon and would have to go to Israel to live with Joseph. I confessed to her that I was not surprised by her admission of my adoption -- I had always suspected as much -- and I reassured her that I had no intention of embracing as a father a man who wanted nothing to do with me until I represented financial gain for him.

I remember nothing about the court proceedings other than sitting in the witness box and looking out at a short, rotund, gray-haired, balding man in a shiny silver-gray herringbone suit. When the judge asked me whether I recognized this man as my father, I replied, "No, Your Honor. This is not my father. The only father I have ever known and want to know is the man who has loved me and cared for me all these years," and I pointed to Leon. In my mind, a father was defined as "the male elder who attended one's passage from childhood to adulthood," the person whose "presence in my life had been a constant... [who] had borne witness," as Wally Lamb expressed it in *I Know This Much Is True*. DNA may determine paternity, but biology has very little to do with parenthood. Nurturing, sheltering, protecting, caring, disciplining, teaching -- in short, raising a child is what defines a parent. How did I feel as I denounced the man whose genes I shared? Eda had told me how readily Joseph had abandoned me (as well as another wife and child; more on that later). I felt nervous and anxious, but I had only resentment for this man who, now that I was a young adult and did not require much care, wanted to tear me away from the only family I had ever known, from the life they had helped me to forge for myself, just so he could use me for monetary gain. I don't even know whether he is still alive and to tell the truth, I am not even curious about him -- for the most part. I thought I felt no emotion in connection with this incident, but even just writing about it now has made my hands grow so cold that I can hardly pick out the letters on my keyboard. Maybe I'm not so unfeeling after all...

To get back to Erin's report, I like her description of Eda's physical characteristics: "Gita is a very petite, attractive women [sic] who exudes an energy that is not commensurate with her size. This sprightly, animated woman... prides herself on being able to make people laugh. This skill, she says, she has had her entire life. Her friends in Poland used to say, 'It doesn't matter where we go, as long as Gita is at our table, we will have a good time!' When I inquired about this seemingly enduring trait, Gita told me that this is the only way she can be, because she has 'so much love to give to people' because she was 'given so much love as a child.'" Erin continues: "I asked Gita about her family life in Poland, before the war, but she was reluctant to discuss it, saying only that she was 'always everyone's pet... loved by everyone.'"

On the subject of family, Erin writes: "Gita told me that she and her daughter are very close. They communicate by phone at least once or twice a week and visit each other frequently. Gita also expressed that she takes great pleasure in the relationship she has with her granddaughters. She told me that her granddaughters are almost her 'closest friends.'" Erin notes that "Gita's adoption of the American values of self-sufficiency and independence have affected how she views aging. Gita proudly told me... that she currently takes care of herself without 'bothering' her family at all. Furthermore, she claimed that she would never move in with her daughter if her health began failing because she would never want to become a 'burden.' I played devil's advocate and created some hypothetical situations and asked if in those situations would she consider moving in or taking some form of support from her family. In each situation she replied that she wouldn't, saying 'Why would I want to live with them [her daughter and son-in-law]? They are busy all day and I would be alone. Here [in her apartment] I get along fine and can take care of myself.'" Again, Eda dismissed everything that I had done and continued to do to help her. How did she envision that, should she become incapacitated, she would survive if she refused to move in with me and simultaneously expected me to keep my promise never to put her in a nursing home?

Erin concludes: "My visit with Gita was delightful." Erin was not alone in her opinion; Eda could charm anyone when she put her mind to it. Maybe I have not been entirely fair to Eda. From time to time, I have seen how other people's interpretation of her actions differed from mine. When I finally went in for my first mammogram, I told the doctor, "The only reason I'm here is so that my mother will stop nagging me." She just gave me one of those looks and said, "Your mother loves you." That took the wind out of my sails! When Eda was moving into her apartment, she called me at work and asked me to come over so I could determine which cartons I wanted to take home with me to give to the girls. I told her that I was working and that I would stop by in the afternoon. My boss had overheard my end of the conversation, and he said, "Your mother needs you. Go to her." Even last year, when I was putting the moisturizer that mother liked on her face, she reached out with her one functioning hand and tried to turn back the sleeve of my blouse. I took this to mean that even now, I'm still not getting it right. But when I told the hospice nurse about it, she said, "Isn't that sweet! Your mother really loves you."

I believe that the most important job a parent has, aside from providing for the child's physical comfort, is to instill in the child a sense of worthiness. Eda did not give me this sense of having value and merit. Her own insecurities manifested themselves through her constant need to demonstrate her superiority at other people's expense. She failed me in many ways, but as I struggle with the challenges of being a good mother to my daughters, I have come to realize that she truly did the best she could, especially given the very difficult situation of inheriting her sister's rebellious child under appalling conditions. I am sure that the responsibilities of child care derailed her dreams of being forever young, forever the beautiful belle of the ball.

I have to work hard to maintain a sense of normalcy, of balance. Sometimes I am tempted to use my terrible childhood as an excuse for behaving in an unacceptable manner. I could sit around and whine and feel sorry for myself. I could wallow in survivor guilt. Every time life deals me a bum hand or I make a bad decision and have to face the consequences, I could play the blame game. After all, my childhood was more wretched than most people's. It would be easy for me to slip into depression, given my ever-present feelings of guilt, of inadequacy, incompetence, and unworthiness. If someone does not answer my message or doesn't respond to my greeting or leaves me out of their plans, I immediately jump to the conclusion that I have done something to offend that person. Even though I know that usually there are extenuating circumstances that have nothing to do with me, I can't help putting blame on myself and beating myself up. But whenever I feel myself heading for a pity party, I drive past a hospital. I look at the windows, and I imagine the pain and suffering of the patients in the rooms behind those windows. I am so thankful that I am on the outside, not in one of those hospital rooms! I head home with renewed appreciation for how good my life is and how fortunate I am to have sufficient means to acquire the things that bring beauty into my life and make my daily existence more comfortable. I am grateful that my health allows me to travel, to go hiking, to accomplish tasks with a minimum of pain and discomfort. Most of all, I derive joy from the loved ones who enrich my life and make it worthwhile as well as from those whose memories I cherish.

I have written this section about my relationship with my mother not to malign or to dishonor her or to convey any disrespect for her as a person. My purpose is to explain why this book could not have been written sooner and how I was shaped by Eda's influence. She did the best she was capable of doing. She was also the product of her time and circumstances, and life certainly did not treat her tenderly. During a significant portion of her young adult life, she did not have the luxury of introspection, self-help books, psychiatric counseling, or Xanax. She was too busy trying to survive and to make a home for her little family.

I talk about Eda in the past tense because even though her indomitable survival instinct keeps her organs from shutting down, the essence of Eda died when she had her stroke. Never again will she march down the corridor with determination starching every limb in her little body. Never again will I hear her laugh with childish delight at some saying that tickled her sense of humor. Never again will I hear her tell me how much everybody loves her. Never again will she tell me how to fix my hair, arrange the furniture in my house, or get rid of my wrinkles. I miss all of that...

I had reached this point in my book when I got the call telling me that mother had died. For four years after her death, I was unable to touch this material. I have finally broken through the mental barrier, and I have resumed my writing.

Late in the afternoon of Tuesday, November 10th, I received a telephone call from Eda's nursing home. Apparently she had been her usual self until they tried to get her up for dinner and found that she had died. I jumped into my car and drove to the nursing home and entered her room with unnerving anxiety. For the first time in years, Eda's poor little body was not all twisted up and her face was not contorted in a grimace. She looked peaceful. She was still warm as I smoothed the hair on her forehead and kissed her face. I sat and talked to her for a long time, telling her all the things I wanted her to take away with her. By the time the nurse arrived and all the necessary paperwork had been completed, Eda's body had grown cold, and the finality of her death really hit me. I was overwhelmed by a sense of sadness, but it was a good good-bye. Rest in peace, Eda, you've earned it.

In accordance with her wishes, I held a memorial service for her at my home. A dozen of the white roses she had requested had a prominent place on the table. Her granddaughters recalled some of the times they had spent with her. Cousin Tim recollected an incident that showed what a life force Eda had been. I would like to quote from the eulogy I gave for her to sum up how I wanted my friends to see her: "How do I describe my mother? The words that come to mind are petite, charming, and childlike. Eda never saw herself as old, and she sought out the company of young people. She tried to keep up with all the latest news and fads so that she could converse with her young friends. She kept her mind active at all times, memorizing poems, translating stories into other languages, trying to learn about baseball and computers. She loved to laugh, often at her own witticisms. Maybe because she experienced so much ugliness and horror during the war years, Eda loved beauty -- in nature, in art, in literature, in furniture, in clothes, in people's appearance... She was always fastidious about her dress and her grooming, even to the point of vanity

My mother expected nothing short of perfection from me at all times, and this caused me much distress over the years because I invariably let her down, since I was far from being a perfect daughter. But despite our differences, I miss her more than I imagined I would. Eda liked to present herself as a frail hothouse flower, but there was steel in that perfectly straight spine of hers, and she knew how to use it to get her way and to overcome any obstacles with which life challenged her, to survive. In the end, she wanted what we all want: to be loved, admired, and respected. I'm relieved that her suffering is over and she is finally at peace. I like to picture her sitting up there somewhere, reunited with her beloved husband and all her long-lost relatives and friends, sipping a cup of tea and trading stories about their crazy families."

PART III - WHAT I'VE BEEN TOLD

There is so much I don't know about my family, my heritage, my past, and myself -- so much I will never know. I know nearly nothing about my older brother Wilek. I know nothing about the family history of either of my fathers -- the biological one and the one who raised me. I understand what Mendelsohn meant when he wrote, "... [You] decide, suddenly, that it's important to let your children know where they came from -- you need the information that people you once knew always had to give you, if only you'd asked. But by the time you think to ask, it's too late."

On what date was I born? Was my mother in labor for a long time or was I eager to make my entrance into the world? How long did I stay with my birth parents before I was given to the Polish family? What is my medical family history? There are so many shadows flitting through the background of my consciousness that will never see the light of day because the people who could have enlightened me have either passed away or are no longer able to recall or to communicate the information to me. Eda could have filled in many of the gaps, but we didn't talk about those terrible years until it was almost too late. Why didn't I ask her sooner? I didn't know how to ask the right questions, and whenever I did broach the subject, Eda invariably put me off with, "Someday you'll understand."

There was a prevailing attitude among survivors that "[t]hings kept quiet simply never happened," as Isabel Allende so aptly summed it up in *Daughter of Fortune*. The nightmares "lived on in the limbo of things not given to words." Eda was reluctant to dredge up those painful memories, and I must admit that I didn't press her too hard because I was a willing participant in the conspiracy of silence. I subscribed to the illusion that if you didn't talk about it, if you left things

145

vague and didn't fill in too many of the details, then you wouldn't have to deal with the horror of the reality; you could consign the past to the status of one of those nightmares, those broken dreams. "If it wasn't spoken of, somehow it didn't exist," says Thane Rosenbaum in *Second Hand Smoke*. "Some truths can never be shared, not even among family." When I finally realized that it is important to keep the memories alive, I invited Eda to lunch one day in June 1998, and I asked her, as one adult to another, to tell me everything she could remember. Even then she glossed over any elements that didn't feature her in a flattering spotlight. I meant to follow up at a later date with questions about the things that weren't clear to me, but I never got the chance. Though the details differed somewhat from the bits and pieces I had gleaned over the years, here is what I've been able to piece together from what she told me that day and on previous occasions, as well as what I learned from my aunt Eva. I am aware that some of it is unclear and incomplete, but that is all the information I have.

I was born Brigita Olga Ashengrau (I was called Ola) in November of 1939 (I don't know the exact day). When Eda and Leon adopted me, they changed my birth date to January 5, 1940. Eda told me that she did that because she and Leon were married on January 24, 1938, and since she was passing me off as her daughter, it wasn't "nice" for a wife to become pregnant so soon after her wedding. I suspect she changed the date of my birth for other reasons. For one thing, it would make it more difficult for the "authorities" to find me. This may have been the reason Eda insisted that, rather than getting my citizenship when my parents became naturalized citizens, I waited until I was 18 to take the test; after much study of a dog-eared copy of an entire volume on U.S. history, I became a citizen in my own right, a very proud milestone in my life. I think that, with her fixation on youth and on hiding her real age, Eda believed she was buying some time by having a daughter who was born in a later decade. At any rate, I was born in Drohobycz, a small town on a lake near Borysław, an area that had many big oil wells. According to a web page by Roman Zakharii, before 1939, Drohobych (note the alternate spelling) had a large Jewish minority. It had 35,000 inhabitants then, and 40% were Jews. Jewish presence in Drohobych was first mentioned in the 15th century. In 1939, the town's population was made up of 10,000 Poles, 10,000 Ukrainians, and 15,000 Jews living in an uneasy coexistence. ([During] WW II, Drohobych Jews were sent to Belzec extermination camp. Many of them were killed in the nearby forest of Bronice. 400 remained alive in 1944). The first time I saw the name Drohobycz in print was in an inscription on a stained glass window at the United States Holocaust Memorial Museum. The first time I saw Drohobycz mentioned in a book was in Diane Ackerman's *The Zookeeper's Wife*, in which she cites a "curfew horror story" about the Polish painter and prose writer Bruno Schulz. An article in *The New York Times* talks about how Schulz was shot by a Gestapo officer in 1942 as he crossed a street in *Drogobych* (note the change in spelling when the town belongs to Ukraine), "the provincial Polish home town he hated but could never leave."

Eda's father, Jacob (Jakov) Rapp, owned a big warehouse that sold and leased oil drilling equipment. He was a successful businessman and well liked in the community. Although he was an orthodox Jew and kept a kosher home, he was tolerant and did not insist that his children follow his example. Not overly generous by nature, he did follow his wife's lead in showing generosity to his family. Jacob was married to Rose (Roza, Rusia), whose maiden name was Mersel. She was a housekeeper and worked very hard. She never had any nice clothes or fine things. The couple had five surviving children; apparently they also had a daughter who died at the age of eight (Eda was very vague about this). The oldest was a son named Oscar (Aunt Eva writes that the oldest was named Joshua; I don't know which is correct). Then came the oldest daughter, Matilda (Lala -- my birth mother), then Eda (Edzia), then Samuel (Milek), and Dina (Dunka) was the youngest.

The family, which was highly respected in the community, lived in a house on Mickiewcza Street in an integrated neighborhood, and the siblings played with the children of the town mayor, the doctor, and other professionals (Eda made a point of this to show that they were associated with the upper echelons of society). When they were older, they went out socially in groups. Eda was the middle child. She studied in Lwow (during World War II, this Polish city was seized by Soviet troops; from 1941-44, it was occupied by the German Army; in 1945, the city became part of the Ukranian SSR and was named Lvov; in 1991, the city's name was changed to Lviv), where she completed a two-year college with a degree in business. Upon graduation, Eda was offered a good job.

She met Leon at one of the local dances. At first, she refused to date him because she was popular and had several boyfriends who courted her and even wrote poetry for her. But Leon was persistent and little by little, she began to realize how good and kind he was, so when he proposed to her over dinner one night, she accepted. At that time, he was a student. Leon was from a well-to-do family that made their fortune in the oil refining business in Drohobycz. For her trousseau, Eda received hand-embroidered gowns and lingerie, and the couple were also given a nice home with fine furnishings in Drohobycz, where they lived until the Russians seized that part of Poland to get their hands on the oil resources. Shortly before the outbreak of the war, when the Russians confiscated all their oil mining equipment, Leon's family became destitute. The Russians started taking well-educated, intellectual Polish people to Russia. They offered to send Eda to Odessa to make use of her accounting skills, but she refused to go. At this time, Eda and Leon were living in the home of a lawyer who was taken away to Siberia. On

August 31, 1939, Eda and Leon had made plans to go on vacation with friends. During the night, they heard what sounded like loud thunder. They looked out of the window and saw trucks rolling by, covered with blood and carrying corpses. The Germans had bombed the airport and on September 1, 1939, they were transporting the dead.

The Russians were taking Poles into Russia, so Eda and Leon traveled by train to Russia with a friend, Renia Himmel. The trains were being bombed, and Renia's husband was killed in the bombing. Eda and Leon fled and traveled through Russia and the satellite countries, where Leon worked as a physician. The Germans and Poles started fighting, and the Germans advanced as far as Stalingrad. The Poles were mobilized, and Leon was conscripted into the Polish army and was separated from Eda for more than six months. Here I need to digress for a moment. This is the only time Eda mentioned Leon's conscription into the *Polish* army; in all future communications, she said that he was in the *Russian* army. I wondered about this until I read in my notes that Eda said that America did not admit people who had served in the Polish army. Piecing together all these bits of information, I have reached the conclusion that this was the big lie that caused Eda to fear for the rest of her life that the authorities would find us and deport us. I think that Leon actually served in the Polish army but that, in order to gain entry into the United States, he somehow falsified the papers to say that he had served in the Russian army or to omit any mention of army service altogether. He certainly was not the only one to do so. As stated in the Wikipedia article on HIAS, "throughout the war people had fled from one place to another, escaped from concentration camps to hide in villages and forests, then reappeared under assumed names. Identity papers were destroyed; false papers, fabricated papers, or, most often, no papers at all, were common."

During the time that Leon was in the army, Eda stayed behind in Tashkent, the capital city of what is now Uzbekistan.

While there, she became very sick with worms and had to be taken to the hospital. When she heard that Drohobycz and Boryslaw had been liberated, Eda traveled with two young men to Lwow, where she was put up in a room for the night by an acquaintance, then she went on to Boryslaw to visit the cemetery where her parents were buried. Milek found her there and told her that I was alive, that she should contact her friend Cesia Bakenroder to find me (Cesia and her husband were the ones who had handed me over to the Polish family, so they knew where I was). In the meantime, a friend informed Eda that Leon was still alive. While he was in the Russian (according to Eda) army in occupied Poland, he became gravely ill with typhoid. He went into a deep depression in the hospital, but he eventually recovered and came to Poland, where Eda was waiting for him.

While she was waiting for Leon to make his way from Russia, she traveled by train to where I was hidden. She told me that she was carrying a suitcase that contained Leon's medical diploma from Prague University Medical School. A guard wanted to throw it out of the train, but Eda cried, and he let her keep it. (I found it in her closet when I cleaned out her apartment.) Eda found me and came to talk to me through the bars in the basement window. As soon as Leon arrived, he and Eda met with Juzek, my birth father, and convinced him to let them take me; apparently it didn't take much convincing because Juzek was not eager to be burdened with the responsibility of a young daughter. Juzek had remarried and had a son with his second wife. He sent her back to Russia to get their belongings, and in the meantime, he ran away to Israel with his son, abandoning his wife, who never saw him again.

Leon and Eda sold all their possessions and gave what money they could raise to the Polish family that had harbored me, convincing them that Leon was a doctor and therefore could provide me with an education and a good upbringing. Leon went to Warsaw to convince the commanding officer in charge to release him from service in the Polish army because he and his wife were the sole survivors of the family and he was needed to help raise a daughter. He was granted a discharge, and so I went to live with my adopted parents. Eda has told me that it's a good thing she found me when I was still so young because if I had stayed with the Polish family longer, it is likely that I would have been abused sexually by the alcoholic husband. Indeed, in an article entitled *Jewish Victims of the Holocaust: Hidden Children*, I read that because they could not turn to local authorities for help or were afraid of being turned out, some children had to endure physical or sexual abuse by their "protectors."

Now to backtrack: Matilda, known as Lala, was my birth mother. She was olive-skinned and had dark eyes and dark hair. Though heavy-set, she was attractive. She was the oldest daughter and, as her mother's favorite, she was dressed beautifully by Rose, who prevailed upon Jacob to spend the money for these clothes. She was very stubborn (evidently a hereditary trait!) and fought a lot with her older brother Milek. She was sent to a boarding school in Lwow, where she finished *gymnasium* (academic high school for students going on to a university). At a young age (23 or 24), she entered into an arranged marriage with Juzek Ashengrau. His parents, who owned a mill, were nice people. But he was not a "local yokel," and it was not a happy marriage. Their first-born was a son who died from encephalitis (inflammation of the brain) or meningitis (inflammation of the protective layers covering the brain and spinal cord) -- I heard both versions from Eda -- at the outbreak of the war when he was five years old (I also heard that he died at age three or four by falling off his high chair and hitting his head). This brother whom I never knew, Wilek, was the apple of Lala's eye, and I can only imagine her grief at losing him. When the war broke out, Cesia Bakenroder and her husband gave me to a Polish couple who was childless.

Cesia's brother sent them provisions from time to time until he was killed in the war; Cesia eventually settled in Canada. She was the one who told Eda where to find me when the war was over. I never found out how Lala, my birth mother, was killed; I only know that she didn't survive the war.

From all reports, Eda's sister Dina (Dunka), the baby of the family, was a stunning beauty, with flaming red hair and gorgeous eyes. Rumor has it that during the German occupation, she was standing at the railway station with her parents when a German SS soldier made a pass at her. She spat in his face. Here the story has two versions. In one she was tortured to death, pulled apart nail by nail, finger by finger, limb by limb to serve as an example of what happens to Jews who show insubordination to the Germans. In the other version, the German officer shot her on the spot. Either way, she also did not survive the war.

Milek (Eda's brother Samuel) was in Stalingrad at this time and was unable to get out. Eda and Leon sent him a Longines watch that Eda had received from her father and some money, which enabled him to buy his way out. He traveled to Ulm (a city in southwestern Germany whose claim to fame is a church with the tallest tower in the world, almost the only structure left standing after the bombing), where we met him after we left the DP camp in Austria. Because he was an engineer, a profession not considered to be essential, Milek could not gain entry into the U.S., so after spending a couple of weeks with us in Gauting, he traveled to Australia. There he met and married Eva Gorzalczany. They had one son, Jim, who still lives in Melbourne.

I know of one other relative who survived the war: Eda's first cousin, David Graubert. At the time we were in the DP camp near Vienna, David was the dean of a university in Holland. He was searching for us and apparently rode his motorcycle into the DP camp where we were living, but for some reason he was unable to find us (perhaps he was searching under Rapp, Eda's maiden name, while she had taken Leon's name of Zwilling. This is one of the questions I wish I could have asked Eda to clarify.)

When we left Ulm, we traveled to Gauting, a suburb of Munich in southern Germany. From Wikipedia I learned that "[a]fter the war, the special military hospital for tuberculosis, situated in a former barracks building, was used in 1945 for treating the survivors of the concentration camps by the US Forces. Since many of the casualties were Jewish, a separate Jewish Cemetery was established in Gauting, next to the main cemetery." This may well be the reason Leon decided to go to Gauting, since tuberculosis was his specialty. I assume that this was the hospital where he worked as a doctor and where we lived (another question I wish I could have asked mother). My parents were afraid that I would be contaminated by the patients, so they found a room in the house of the painter, Paul Hey, as I described in the first part of this book. The sanatorium provided us with food, but from time to time, Eda traveled by train to Munich and to Ulm to get provisions on the black market.

After two years in Gauting, Leon's Uncle David Zwilling sent him an affidavit vouching for his character and guaranteeing financial support. Leon also had an affidavit from the Physicians' Association, which brought us over. Prof. Hey also wrote a couple of letters in support of Leon's application for a visa, but no one could read Gothic script, so Eda threw the letters away (here again I have a question: did she throw the letters away because it was politically dangerous to have such letters from a German?). In September 1949, we sailed out of Bremerhaven on the *General C. C. Ballou* . I described our journey in Part I, but Eda told me one additional little story: to combat seasickness, they gave us celery. I had never eaten it before, and I was fascinated by this odd vegetable.

When we finally arrived on the shores of "the land of milk and honey, whose streets are paved with gold," it turned out that Eda had high blood pressure and the authorities didn't want to admit her, but Leon got her into the country (I wish I knew how). Upon our arrival in New York City, we were met by a representative of the Physicians' Committee, who took us to our hotel in a taxi. The Committee paid for us to stay in a small room in the hotel (I seem to remember that we stayed in more than one hotel) for one month, then we moved into the one-bedroom, low-rent apartment of a friend who had just moved out. Polio was rampant in the city, so after Leon received his license to practice medicine, we moved to Clinton, a small town in upstate New York. A physician in Syracuse set Leon up in practice; Leon paid him off gradually. This is where the information ends and, since everyone who could supply more facts (David, Leon, Milek, Eda, and Eva) has passed away, this is where I must end my story. The effects of the war become less acute over time, but nonetheless, they will persist for generations to come.

ADDENDUM

When I came home from playing mah jongg on Wednesday, February 26, 2014, my husband told me that there was a call from my brother. Confused, I said, "I don't have a brother!" Curiosity got the better of me, so I called the number that Bob handed me. I was convinced that this was a scam, that sooner or later I would be hit up for a "loan," so I vowed not to reveal any information about myself.

The woman who answered the phone identified herself as Rosalie, the wife of my half-brother. She said that they had been searching for me for years and he was anxious to meet me, so if I wouldn't mind, she would put him on the phone. I agreed, and a male with a slight accent introduced himself to me as Zvi Ben-Joseph. The name got my attention because I knew that in Hebrew, "ben" signifies "son of" and Joseph was my biological father's name. I asked a few questions, but I said very little. I just listened as Zvi told me things about himself and about his family during and after the war that he could only know from experience -- he could not have found these details on Google or in any other source. He even described a picture he had of me wearing ice skates on the back lawn of our house in Clinton that he claimed to have gotten from "our" father. When I asked him how he had found me, he said that his wife, who knew my adoptive father's name, had been trying for a long time to find my married name and had finally found it in his obituary, which had appeared in the St. Louis newspaper. I was puzzled and still distrustful, so I told him that I preferred to correspond by email. I gave him my email address and asked him to send me photos. The pictures he sent of himself and his family left little doubt that he was who he claimed to be. In particular, he sent a passport picture of my -- our! -- father that made me

155

think of a picture I had of myself at around age six. When I put my picture next to my father's, the resemblance was striking. Little by little, we started corresponding by telephone and email. It turned out that he lives in Moraga, CA. Since Bob and I had been planning to visit our dear friends in Monterey, CA, in June, we coordinated the dates so that we could drive to Moraga to meet him and his family. As time went on, my excitement mounted. My thoughts were so filled with this current of events that I told the story to all my friends. Everyone who heard it was fascinated and wanted to know how things would work out.

At last, June 19th arrived, and we drove to the address Zvi had given us. With my heart in my throat, I knocked on the door. The couple who opened the door was so warm and welcoming and completely unpretentious that it took less than five minutes before we all felt as if we had known each other our entire lives. We chatted non-stop all afternoon and through dinner.

Zvi had told me that he had a friend named Lili Gartner Nelson, who had known our family during and after the war and who could probably fill in some background for me and answer some of my questions. Lili was married to Chuck Nelson, who had written down Lili's account of how she had survived the Holocaust. Chuck had sent me a copy of this memoir, and when I read it, I was struck by the many similarities of our experiences. Lili had lost all her relatives except her father, and she was also hidden by a Polish Catholic family; she, too, spent time in a DP camp in Austria before coming to America. Lili was eager to meet me, and since she and Chuck live in Santa Monica, they drove up to Moraga and joined us after dinner. The conversation flowed easily, and it was well after midnight before we parted, to continue the following day.

Rosie and Zvi have a son, Phil, and a daughter, Leila, each of whom has two children. I got to meet my nephew, who lives in Laguna Hills and is the V.P. of Technology for a marketing firm, when he arrived the following morning. Since Leila is the Technical Training Project Manager for Pixar Animation Studios, we met her at Pixar and she gave us a tour of the studio. We also got to meet some of Rosie and Zvi's friends and neighbors at a party that they threw for us. I can't begin to describe how unaffected and genuine and caring everyone was, and how readily we were accepted into the group. Let me add here that Bob approached the family meeting with a very negative attitude. He does not like to make small talk with a room full of people he doesn't know. Much to my surprise, they won him over completely, and I was the one who dragged him out the door each evening!

From Lili I learned that much of what I had been told about my biological father was not true. I had heard that able-bodied men were conscripted into the Russian army or sent to work in war industries deep in Russia, so I assumed that this was why Joseph (Juzek) was separated from my mother. Juzek was actually driving trucks in the Ural, a skill that was uncommon in that era. It was true that he had a child in Russia in 1942 with another woman. That child, originally named Eugeniusz Ashengrau, is my half-brother, Zvi. The woman, named Maria, was a devout Catholic, and Lili thinks Juzek might have married her while he was still married to my biological mother. I was hoping that Lili would be able to tell me something about my birth mother and what happened to her, but unfortunately Lili did not remember anything about her.

After the war, Juzek, along with Maria and Zeniu (diminutive of Eugeniusz) returned to the family's hometown, Stary Sambor. When the war ended in 1945, Stary Sambor became the gathering place for survivors, all looking for relatives and friends who might have survived the Holocaust. It was like a fraternity in exile. Lili thinks that when my adoptive parents found me, this is where they brought me during the few months before we left Poland.

According to Lili, Maria became homesick for her family, so Juzek told her to go back to Russia to visit them. Before she returned, the Russians, who had re-occupied eastern Poland, kicked all the Jews out of Galicia (now Ukraine), including Stary Sambor, and sent them to live in Walbrzych, a German town located on an eastern sliver of Germany which, by Soviet decree, became part of Poland. When Maria came back to Stary Sambor, she searched for Juzek and the baby, but she could not find them. She gave a silver cross to Lili's father, who was still in Stary Sambor, and asked him to give it to her son if he ever saw Zeniu again.

In the meantime, Juzek was unable to care for the baby by himself, so he put him in an orphanage in Walbrzych. Shortly thereafter, Juzek met a woman named Ziuta Waisbrot, who had also been kicked out of Galicia by the Soviets. In the summer of 1945, Juzek and Ziuta took three-year old Zeniu out of the orphanage, and Juzek married Ziuta. Juzek started dealing with the Russians, buying and selling truck parts. Together with some friends, he started a transportation company in Walbrzych, which grew and became successful.

During our visit in Moraga with my new-found family, we ate and drank, we hiked and hugged, we talked and laughed, but regardless of what was on the agenda for each day, I insisted on spending some time alone with Zvi so that he could tell me about himself. This is the story he told me.

Zeniu started school in Walbrzych in 1949, and he stayed there through middle school. The family talked about leaving Poland because anti-Semitism was still prevalent there, but they hesitated too long. At the end of 1949, the Russians closed the borders and all emigration was stopped.

When the borders were reopened in 1957, the family left Poland for Israel. Their train went through Vienna to the Italian seaport of Genova, where they had to wait for a week before they could board a ship bound for Israel.

A cousin had arranged for them to be settled in temporary housing in Tiberius (Tveria in Hebrew). During the ride from Haifa to Tveria, they marveled at the large size of the country. Seeing Jewish policemen, Jewish soldiers, and Jewish bus drivers made them proud to be Jewish, unlike being Jewish in Poland, surrounded by anti-Semitism. One important decision was made on the drive to Tveria: Zeniu asked what his name would be in Hebrew, and he arrived in Tveria with his new Hebrew name of Zvi, which means "deer." Zeniu (now Zvi) started working on a kibbutz, where he studied Hebrew in the mornings and worked at assigned jobs in the afternoons.

A year after his arrival in Israel, Zvi interviewed at the Technical Institute of the Air Force in Haifa and was ultimately admitted, even though he lacked the required two years of high school. After two years, he finished the equivalent of high school and graduated as a technician of jet and piston-engine planes.

Upon graduating from the Institute, he joined the military, and in 1959, he was assigned to a squadron of cargo planes as an airplane mechanic. Eventually he progressed to the status of flight engineer. This position entailed frequent flights to Europe. When he started flying abroad, he was asked by operations if he would mind changing his name to an Israeli-sounding one, since he was essentially an ambassador of Israel. With his father's approval, he adopted the name of Zvi Ben-Joseph (son of Joseph in Hebrew); that is the name he goes by to this day.

In pursuit of a better life, Zvi got a job in Israeli Aircraft Industries (IAI), which had a contract with the U.S. Air Force to maintain cargo planes. When he attained the position of test flight engineer for IAI, he realized that there was no room for advancement in this area, and because it was not enough for him to be a "grease monkey," he decided to go to America in order to get a degree.

Since Ziuta was already in New York at this time, she sent Zvi an affidavit so that he would be admitted into the States.

He was accepted into the mechanical engineering curriculum of the New York Institute of Technology (NY Tech). For one semester he worked part-time after school. During the following semester, he went to night school and worked full-time as a draftsman in the electrical department of a large company. This job lasted until he graduated with a B.S. degree in mechanical engineering in 1974.

A friend of the family, Lola Welgreen, was the one who helped him find an apartment in Manhattan, and her husband Julius helped him find his first engineering job, so Zvi was a frequent visitor in their home. When he met their daughter Rosalie, she was only 16, and they became good friends. As time went on, they started dating and fell in love. Zvi and Rosalie were married in December 1967.

Rosalie attended Music and Art High School and entered Hunter College in the fall of 1967. She decided to continue college at night, and eventually she obtained a B.A. degree in Economics. A few months after the wedding, Zvi got an offer from a firm of engineering consultants as an electrical designer at a much higher salary. He stayed with this company for four years. Their son Phillip was born in 1971, and daughter Leila came along only 18 months later, in 1972.

After a series of jobs with various companies, Zvi decided to become an electrical contractor. His timing was bad because the economy had soured and there were no jobs for contractors. He got his Professional Engineer license, a prestigious designation. He worked at a few jobs until he saw an ad for licensed electrical and mechanical engineers in a company that was opening an office in San Francisco. In 1979, Zvi accepted the position, and his family joined him in 1980. They decided to live in Moraga, where they rented and then bought a house in which they lived until 2003.

Zvi worked at this company until 1985, and then he started his own business. Little by little, his company -- Pacific Engineering Associates -- acquired gainful projects and continued to flourish. In 2000, he sold the company but stayed on as a principal for two years. He retired in 2002 and took up golf, so he and Rosalie bought a house near a golf course. When he is not golfing, he helps out with the grandchildren. Rosalie still does some consulting for Tocara Jewelry.

In 1977-78, Juzek tried to claim me so that he could collect reparations. According to Zvi, my adoptive father Leon did everything he could to discourage him. As I've related earlier, Juzek went so far as to take us to court. After I repudiated him, gentle, mild-mannered Leon read him the riot act and told him in no uncertain terms that Juzek was never, ever to try to contact me again or there would be harsh consequences. Now I wonder whether the changes that Eda and Leon made in names, dates, and places were motivated -- at least in part -- by their wish to keep Juzek from finding me.

Bob and I both remarked that in his appearance as well as his mannerisms, Zvi reminds us of Leon. He is easy-going, gentle, self-effacing, has a positive outlook on life and a dry sense of humor. Rosie, on the other hand, is a dynamo. If you so much as mention something that you've thought about doing, she'll make it happen -- almost before the words are out of your mouth. She is a bundle of energy, and she draws people to her with her cheerful disposition. I feel incredibly fortunate that she found me and that I now have such a wonderful family in my life. I am looking forward to many frequent exchanges and enjoyable reunions. So many tragic losses, and then -- one miraculous find.

AFTERWORD

This book was difficult for me to write. It is hard for me to dredge up so many painful memories that have lain dormant in my subconscious for years and years. Not only do I get depressed when I read stories about the Holocaust or see movies about it or even think about anything associated with it, I have actual physical reactions: accelerated heartbeat, shortness of breath, cold sweat, restlessness, and general malaise. I also start having nightmares -- broken dreams. That is why I was hesitant to go to the United States Holocaust Memorial Museum when it first opened in Washington, DC. My dear friend Aline, who came to DC for my daughter Ami's wedding, and my older daughter Lisa, also there for the wedding, volunteered to go with me for moral support and to leave with me if I became overwhelmed. As we walked through the numerous exhibits, I was overcome with a plethora of emotions, but I was holding my own as part of the subdued group making its way through the museum. At one point, I heard someone sniffling behind me, and the sniffling grew louder and increasingly annoying, disturbing the reverential silence. Thinking "I wish that person would use a Kleenex or a handkerchief," I turned around -- only to see my Lisa sobbing uncontrollably. She had just seen the video of the soldiers liberating Auschwitz concentration camp, and she had suddenly realized, "Dear God, my Aunt Eva is one of those people!" With that realization, all the stories she had heard about other people took on a terrible, frightening, immediately personal reality. (In point of fact, Eva was in another camp at the time of the Allied liberation, since she was shuffled around to three different concentration camps and endured unimaginable suffering, but that is a whole other book.)

My undoing came in a different part of the museum. I was most deeply affected by the area where the children told their stories. One day they were playing with their friends, giggling and sharing stories or competing in sports. The next day these same friends were not permitted to talk to them or play with them. The following day the Jewish children were not allowed to go to school at all. And they asked themselves, "What did we do wrong? Why are we being punished?" For unlike adults, children do not understand discrimination and hate based on religion or skin color. As the song from *The King and I* goes, "You've got to be taught to hate and fear."

Recently I heard a speech by Paul Rusesabagina, the acting manager of the *Hotel des Milles Collines*, who is credited with saving more than 1200 refugees during the Rwandan Genocide; his story is the subject of the movie *Hotel Rwanda*. I was struck by his account of how at one point, when he was in college, his best friend warned Paul that something might happen to him because the decades-long rivalry between the Tutsis and the Hutus was heating up. Sure enough, one day his friend did disappear and Paul never saw him again -- simply because he belonged to the wrong tribe. And the ultimate irony is that Paul himself is half Tutsi and half Hutu; it just so happened that he and his father were both classified as Hutus and were thus on the "correct" side of the conflict! How is it possible that so many lives can hang in the balance on something so arbitrary?

And so we say "never again," but even as we say the words, we know in our heart of hearts that it has happened and is happening and will continue to happen again and again and again -- in Africa, in Europe, and -- perhaps with less publicity -- in other parts of the world. Maybe it won't be on the same scale, but to a survivor mourning the loss of children and siblings and parents and a spouse -- a whole family of loved ones -- it matters little whether those murdered number in the millions or the thousands or the hundreds.

Ever since I read William Golding's *Lord of the Flies*, I have been haunted by this tale of a group of young boys stranded on an island. Although they realized that they must work together to stay alive, they soon split into two factions under different leaders and before long, the growing hostility between them led to fighting among the boys, with terrible consequences. This novel is the most cogent-- and frightening -- -allegory I have ever encountered of why men can't live in peaceful coexistence.

I experienced a variant of this phenomenon first-hand when I was working in the Office of Research in Medical Education at the University of Texas Medical Branch in Galveston. During one weekend, we all participated in a faculty/staff development workshop under the auspices of the A. K. Rice Institute for the Study of Social Systems, whose mission, as stated on their web site, is to "facilitate learning by doing, being, thinking and feeling within a 'group relations conference' event. This experiential approach helps us identify the often hidden, unexamined or unconscious aspects of how we live and work in groups and organizations." Following a meeting to brief us on the structure of the conference, we were divided into groups, and each group was assigned a task (we later learned that the tasks were simply a pretext to initiate the group interaction). The members of each group lost no time in establishing rules and regulations, thus attaining some degree of cohesiveness. What astonished me was how quickly each of the groups began to turn against the others. I wanted to sample the atmosphere in several of the groups before I chose a group with which I wanted to work during the entire weekend. To my astonishment, I was made to sit in the back of the room and I was not allowed to participate in any of the discussions or to cast any votes until I made a firm commitment to join that group. It was surprisingly disconcerting to be treated like an unwelcome outsider, almost like an alien.

In the course of the year, several coworkers had formed a so-called staff development group, the "e-club," which would meet from time to time on a Friday afternoon at someone's home; the only requirement for membership in this group was that you had to be an employe"e" (as opposed to an employe"r.") On the second day of the A. K. Rice workshop, several members of the "e-club" decided to go out for lunch. Upon our return, we were met with hostility that was downright palpable. Nowhere in the guidelines for the weekend was there any prohibition against going off campus, but somehow we were perceived as having broken some unwritten taboo, resulting in resentment and even open verbal aggression. How could this be happening? After all, these were my friends, my colleagues with whom I interacted amicably on a daily basis. If it was so easy in so short a time to manipulate intelligent, well-educated, professional colleagues into taking an antagonistic stance against each other, then it is not hard to understand how a charismatic leader, given enough time and resources, could incite a disgruntled populace into committing acts of murder and brutality. This we must never forget.

In our need to belong, to be *included*, we tend to forget that there are then others who must perforce be *excluded*. And from exclusion, it is only a few short steps to persecution and, ultimately, to execution. This process will continue as long as the nature of men remains unchanged. And here I use the masculine gender deliberately, for I believe (as do those who have conducted numerous studies on the subject and have traced the origin back to the role of man as warrior/protector/hunter) that, with few exceptions, it is the male of the species who is inclined to settle disputes through physical combat. A man sees vulnerability and he perceives a creature to be conquered and vanquished. A woman sees vulnerability and she perceives a creature to be nurtured and rehabilitated. Reduced to its most basic components, it's testosterone versus estrogen.

I feel it is important for me to get my story out because whether this little volume ends up in a book store, in a small Holocaust museum, or on a dusty attic shelf, I can only hope that somehow, somewhere, it will wind up in the hands of someone who will be moved to say, "Maybe the Holocaust really *did* happen, and maybe enough is enough…"

BIBLIOGRAPHY

A. K. Rice Institute. <http://akriceinstitute.org/>

Ackerman, Diane. *The Zookeeper's Wife.* New York: W.W. Norton & Company, Inc., 2007.

Allende, Isabel. *Daughter of Fortune: A Novel.* New York: HarperCollins Publishers, 1999.

Anderson, Joan. *A Walk on the Beach: Tales of Wisdom From an Unconventional Woman.* New York: Broadway Books, 2004.

Binchy, Maeve. *Light a Penny Candle.* New York: Dell Publishing Company, Inc., 1982.

Binford, Mira Reym and Hank Heifetz. *Diamonds in the Snow.* Documentary film. Directed by Mira Reym Binford. 10 April 1994.

Camp Ranger: Friendship and Memories to Last a Lifetime. <http://www.campranger.com/>

Carter, Stephen L. *The Emperor of Ocean Park.* New York: Alfred A. Knopf, 2002.

Clinton Comets. <http://en.wikipedia.org/wiki/Clinton_Comets>

Cohen, Henry. *The Anguish of the Holocaust Survivors.* Talk at Conservative Synagogue of Fifth Avenue on Yom HaShoah (Holocaust Remembrance Day), April 13, 1996.

Diamant, Anita. *The Red Tent.* New York: Picador, 1997.

Erdrich, Louise. *The Painted Drum.* New York: Harper Collins Publishers, 2005.

Fitch, Janet. *White Oleander.* Boston: Little, Brown and Company, 1999.

Frederiksson, Marianne. *Hanna's Daughters: A Novel*. New York: Ballantine Books, 1994.

Fremont, Helen. *After Long Silence: A Memoir*. New York: Dell Publishing, 1999.

Guterson, David. *Snow Falling on Cedars*. New York: Harcourt, Brace, and Company, 1994.

Golding, William. *Lord of the Flies*. New York: The Berkley Publishing Group,1954.

Gottman, John and Joan DeClaire. *The Relationship Cure: A Five-Step Guide to Strengthening Your Marriage, Family, and Friendships*. New York: Three Rivers Press, 2001.

Hamilton: A National Leader. <http://www.campranger.com/>

HIAS: The Displaced Persons. <http://en.wikipedia.org/wiki/HIAS>

Holland, Agnieszka, Director. *Europa Europa*. World Films, 1990. *Jewish Victims of the Holocaust: Hidden Children*. <http://www.jewishvirtuallibrary.org/jsource/Holocaust/hidden.html>

Kaufman, Michael T. "The Rebirth of a Writer Slain by a Nazi in Poland." *The New York Times* (July 14, 1998)

Lamb, Wally. *I Know This Much Is True*. New York: HarperCollins, 1998.

Mace, Nancy L. and Peter V. Rabins. *The 36-Hour Day: A Family Guide to Caring for People Who Have Alzheimer Disease, Related Dementias, and Memory Loss in Later Life*. Baltimore: The Johns Hopkins University Press, 1981.

Maugham, W. Somerset. *Of Human Bondage*. New York: Bantam Books, 1991.

Mendelsohn, Daniel. *The Lost: A Search for Six of Six Million*. New York: Harper Collins Publishers, 2006.

Nelson, Liliana Gartner. *Little Girl Hidden: How I Survived the Holocaust*. As Told to Chuck Nelson. Private Manuscript.

Rosenbaum, Thane. *Second Hand Smoke*. New York: St. Martin's Press, 1999.

Roth, Henry. *Mercy of a Rude Stream: A Star Shines Over Mt. Morris Park*. New York: Picador, 1994.

Zakharii, Roman. <http://www.personal.ceu.hu/students/97/Roman_Zakharii /drohobych.htm>

ACKNOWLEDGMENTS

A million thanks to my friends, Carol Ellis and Jackie Lipsitz, who carefully proofread the first draft of my manuscript and made many helpful suggestions for improvement. Marilyn Son's unflagging encouragement motivated me to keep working on my book, even when the last thing I wanted to do was to sit down at my computer and write. In her own gentle way, Katharine McGee prompted me to cut out passages that sounded whiney when I looked at them from a reader's point of view. My husband Bob not only gave me the support I needed but also managed to spot a few typos and inconsistencies. And last, but certainly not least, Angela Hoyt, co-owner of BookLocker.com, guided me through the publication procedure and, with her enthusiasm and helpfulness, made the entire process much more pleasant than I had anticipated.

CPSIA information can be obtained
at www.ICGtesting.com
Printed in the USA
BVOW08s0545080917
494271BV00001B/68/P